# Autodesk® Inventor® 2018
# Working with Imported Data

*Student Guide*
*Mixed Units - 1<sup>st</sup> Edition*

Authorized Publisher

# ASCENT - Center for Technical Knowledge®
## Autodesk® Inventor® 2018
## Working with Imported Data
Mixed Units - 1st Edition

Prepared and produced by:

ASCENT Center for Technical Knowledge
630 Peter Jefferson Parkway, Suite 175
Charlottesville, VA 22911

866-527-2368
www.ASCENTed.com

Lead Contributor: Jennifer MacMillan

ASCENT - Center for Technical Knowledge is a division of Rand Worldwide, Inc., providing custom developed knowledge products and services for leading engineering software applications. ASCENT is focused on specializing in the creation of education programs that incorporate the best of classroom learning and technology-based training offerings.

We welcome any comments you may have regarding this student guide, or any of our products. To contact us please email: feedback@ASCENTed.com.

The following are registered trademarks or trademarks of Autodesk, Inc., and/or its subsidiaries and/or affiliates in the USA and other countries: 123D, 3ds Max, Alias, ATC, AutoCAD LT, AutoCAD, Autodesk, the Autodesk logo, Autodesk 123D, Autodesk Homestyler, Autodesk Inventor, Autodesk MapGuide, Autodesk Streamline, AutoLISP, AutoSketch, AutoSnap, AutoTrack, Backburner, Backdraft, Beast, BIM 360, Burn, Buzzsaw, CADmep, CAiCE, CAMduct, Civil 3D, Combustion, Communication Specification, Configurator 360, Constructware, Content Explorer, Creative Bridge, Dancing Baby (image), DesignCenter, DesignKids, DesignStudio, Discreet, DWF, DWG, DWG (design/logo), DWG Extreme, DWG TrueConvert, DWG TrueView, DWGX, DXF, Ecotect, Ember, ESTmep, FABmep, Face Robot, FBX, Fempro, Fire, Flame, Flare, Flint, ForceEffect, FormIt 360, Freewheel, Fusion 360, Glue, Green Building Studio, Heidi, Homestyler, HumanIK, i-drop, ImageModeler, Incinerator, Inferno, InfraWorks, Instructables, Instructables (stylized robot design/logo), Inventor, Inventor HSM, Inventor LT, Lustre, Maya, Maya LT, MIMI, Mockup 360, Moldflow Plastics Advisers, Moldflow Plastics Insight, Moldflow, Moondust, MotionBuilder, Movimento, MPA (design/logo), MPA, MPI (design/logo), MPX (design/logo), MPX, Mudbox, Navisworks, ObjectARX, ObjectDBX, Opticore, P9, Pier 9, Pixlr, Pixlr-o-matic, Productstream, Publisher 360, RasterDWG, RealDWG, ReCap, ReCap 360, Remote, Revit LT, Revit, RiverCAD, Robot, Scaleform, Showcase, Showcase 360, SketchBook, Smoke, Socialcam, Softimage, Spark & Design, Spark Logo, Sparks, SteeringWheels, Stitcher, Stone, StormNET, TinkerBox, Tinkercad, Tinkerplay, ToolClip, Topobase, Toxik, TrustedDWG, T-Splines, ViewCube, Visual LISP, Visual, VRED, Wire, Wiretap, WiretapCentral, XSI.

NASTRAN is a registered trademark of the National Aeronautics Space Administration.

All other brand names, product names, or trademarks belong to their respective holders.

General Disclaimer:

Notwithstanding any language to the contrary, nothing contained herein constitutes nor is intended to constitute an offer, inducement, promise, or contract of any kind. The data contained herein is for informational purposes only and is not represented to be error free. ASCENT, its agents and employees, expressly disclaim any liability for any damages, losses or other expenses arising in connection with the use of its materials or in connection with any failure of performance, error, omission even if ASCENT, or its representatives, are advised of the possibility of such damages, losses or other expenses. No consequential damages can be sought against ASCENT or Rand Worldwide, Inc. for the use of these materials by any third parties or for any direct or indirect result of that use.

The information contained herein is intended to be of general interest to you and is provided "as is", and it does not address the circumstances of any particular individual or entity. Nothing herein constitutes professional advice, nor does it constitute a comprehensive or complete statement of the issues discussed thereto. ASCENT does not warrant that the document or information will be error free or will meet any particular criteria of performance or quality. In particular (but without limitation) information may be rendered inaccurate by changes made to the subject of the materials (i.e. applicable software). Rand Worldwide, Inc. specifically disclaims any warranty, either expressed or implied, including the warranty of fitness for a particular purpose.

# Contents

# Preface

The *Autodesk® Inventor® 2018: Working with Imported Geometry* student guide teaches you how to work with data from other CAD platforms using the Autodesk Inventor software.

Using this student guide, you will learn the various methods for importing data into Autodesk Inventor and how you can edit both imported solid and surface data. Additionally, you will learn how to index scanned point cloud data, and attach and use it in an Inventor file. The final chapters in this student guide discuss how you can use AutoCAD .DWG files in the Autodesk Inventor software.

The topics covered in this student guide are also covered in ASCENT's *Autodesk® Inventor® 2018: Advanced Part Modeling* student guide, which includes a broader range of advanced learning topics.

## Objectives

- Import CAD data into the Autodesk Inventor software.

- Export CAD data from the Autodesk Inventor software in an available export format.

- Index a supported point cloud data file, attach, and edit it for use in a file.

- Use the Edit Base Solid environment to edit solids that have been imported into the Autodesk Inventor software.

- Create Direct Edit features in a model that move, resize, scale, rotate, and delete existing geometry in both imported and native Autodesk Inventor files.

- Set the import options to import surface data from other file format types.

- Transfer imported surface data into the Repair Environment to conduct a quality check for errors.

- Appropriately set the stitch tolerance value so that gaps in the imported geometry can be automatically stitched and identify the gaps that are not stitched.

- Use the Repair Environment commands to repair gaps or delete, extend, replace, trim and break surfaces to successfully create a solid from the imported geometry.

- Open an AutoCAD DWG file directly into an Autodesk Inventor part file and review the data.

- Use the DWG/DXF File Wizard and its options to import files into an Autodesk Inventor file.

- Use an AutoCAD DWG file in an Autodesk Inventor part file so that the geometry created in Inventor remains associative with the AutoCAD DWG file.

### Note on Software Setup

This student guide assumes a standard installation of the software using the default preferences during installation. Lectures and practices use the standard software templates and default options for the Content Libraries.

### Students and Educators can Access Free Autodesk Software and Resources

Autodesk challenges you to get started with free educational licenses for professional software and creativity apps used by millions of architects, engineers, designers, and hobbyists today. Bring Autodesk software into your classroom, studio, or workshop to learn, teach, and explore real-world design challenges the way professionals do.

Get started today - register at the Autodesk Education Community and download one of the many Autodesk software applications available.

Visit www.autodesk.com/joinedu/

*Note: Free products are subject to the terms and conditions of the end-user license and services agreement that accompanies the software. The software is for personal use for education purposes and is not intended for classroom or lab use.*

## Lead Contributor: Jennifer MacMillan

With a dedication for engineering and education, Jennifer has spent over 20 years at ASCENT managing courseware development for various CAD products. Trained in Instructional Design, Jennifer uses her skills to develop instructor-led and web-based training products as well as knowledge profiling tools.

Jennifer has achieved the Autodesk Certified Professional certification for Inventor and is also recognized as an Autodesk Certified Instructor (ACI). She enjoys teaching the training courses that she authors and is also very skilled in providing technical support to end-users.

Jennifer holds a Bachelor of Engineering Degree as well as a Bachelor of Science in Mathematics from Dalhousie University, Nova Scotia, Canada.

Jennifer MacMillan has been the Lead Contributor for *Autodesk Inventor: Working with Imported Data* since its initial release in 2017.

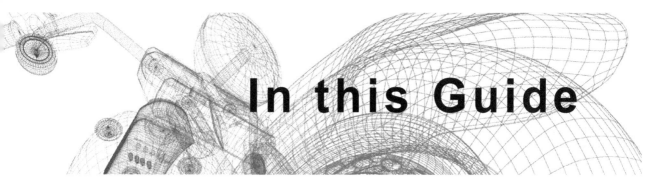

# In this Guide

The following images highlight some of the features that can be found in this Student Guide.

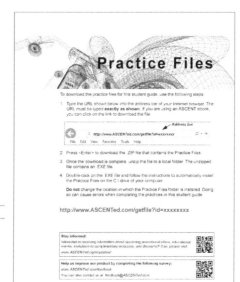

**Practice Files**

The Practice Files page tells you how to download and install the practice files that are provided with this student guide.

*FTP link for practice files*

**Chapters**

Each chapter begins with a brief introduction and a list of the chapter's Learning Objectives.

*Learning Objectives for the chapter*

## Instructional Content

Each chapter is split into a series of sections of instructional content on specific topics. These lectures include the descriptions, step-by-step procedures, figures, hints, and information you need to achieve the chapter's Learning Objectives.

## Side notes

Side notes are hints or additional information for the current topic.

## Practice Objectives

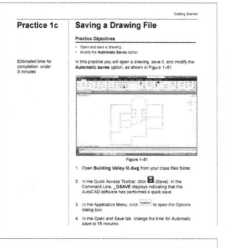

## Practices

Practices enable you to use the software to perform a hands-on review of a topic.

Some practices require you to use prepared practice files, which can be downloaded from the link found on the Practice Files page.

## Chapter Review Questions

Chapter review questions, located at the end of each chapter, enable you to review the key concepts and learning objectives of the chapter.

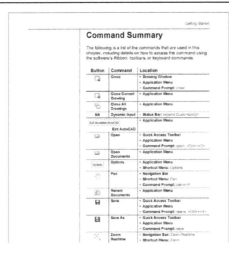

## Command Summary

The Command Summary is located at the end of each chapter. It contains a list of the software commands that are used throughout the chapter, and provides information on where the command is found in the software.

## Icons in this Student Guide

The following icons are used to help you quickly and easily find helpful information.

| | |
|---|---|
| **New** in **2018**  | Indicates items that are new in the Autodesk Inventor 2018 software. |
| **Enhanced** in **2018**  | Indicates items that have been enhanced in the Autodesk Inventor 2018 software. |

# Practice Files

To download the practice files for this student guide, use the following steps:

1. Type the URL shown below into the address bar of your Internet browser. The URL must be typed **exactly as shown**. If you are using an ASCENT ebook, you can click on the link to download the file.

*Address bar*

http://www.ascented.com/getfile?id=maiestas

File    Edit    View    Favorites    Tools    Help

2. Press <Enter> to download the .ZIP file that contains the Practice Files.

3. Once the download is complete, unzip the file to a local folder. The unzipped file contains an .EXE file.

4. Double-click on the .EXE file and follow the instructions to automatically install the Practice Files on the C:\ drive of your computer.

   **Do not** change the location in which the Practice Files folder is installed. Doing so can cause errors when completing the practices in this student guide.

# http://www.ascented.com/getfile?id=maiestas

---

**Stay Informed!**

Interested in receiving information about upcoming promotional offers, educational events, invitations to complimentary webcasts, and discounts? If so, please visit:

*www.ASCENTed.com/updates/*

---

**Help us improve our product by completing the following survey:**

*www.ASCENTed.com/feedback*

You can also contact us at: *feedback@ASCENTed.com*

---

# Chapter
# 1

# Importing CAD Data

The Autodesk® Inventor® software supports the import of files from many different types of 3D CAD programs. In some cases, an associative link can be maintained between the source file and the Autodesk Inventor software. Once a CAD file has been imported, the geometry is brought into an Autodesk Inventor file where it can be further manipulated using tools available in the software. Understanding the editing tools that are available to further manipulate the imported geometry is essential to ensuring the efficient creation of the required model.

## Learning Objectives in this Chapter

- Import CAD data into the Autodesk Inventor software.
- Export CAD data from the Autodesk Inventor software in an available export format.
- Index a supported point cloud data file, attach, and edit it for use in a file.

# 1.1 Importing CAD Data

You can import supported file formats simply by opening the files. The Autodesk Inventor software can open the file formats shown in Figure 1–1.

**Figure 1–1**

## How To: Import Data

1. In the **File** menu or Quick Access Toolbar, select **Open**. The Open dialog box displays.
2. In the Files of type drop-down list, select the file format that is to be imported.
3. Select the file to import and click **Open**. The Import dialog box opens.

---

**Hint: Importing into an Existing File**

You can import CAD Data into existing files using the following options:

- In an open part file, in the *3D Model* tab>Create panel, click ⬆ (Import). The **Import** command is also available on the *Manage* tab>Import panel.

- In an assembly file, in the *Assemble* tab>expanded **Place** commands, click ⬆ (Place Imported CAD Files).

---

- If a part file is imported, a new Autodesk Inventor part file is created.
- If an assembly is imported, a new Autodesk Inventor assembly is created.
- The available options in the dialog box vary depending on the file format that is being imported.

*The imported geometries can be converted or referenced.*

In the example shown in Figure 1–2, a CATIA part file and an .IGS file were selected, as indicated by the filenames at the top of the dialog boxes.

**Figure 1–2**

4. In the *Import Type* area, select how the data will be imported:

- Select **Reference Model** to import the data so that a reference is maintained to the source file. If this option is used, when changes are made to the source file, you can update the model in Autodesk Inventor to reflect the changes.
- Select **Convert Model** to import the geometry and break the link with the original model.

5. In the *Object Filters* area, select the data type to import (i.e., Solids, Surfaces, Meshes, Wires, Work Features, or Points).

6. In the *Inventor Length Units* area, specify the type of length unit to use for the imported geometry. The options enable you to maintain the same units as the data being imported (**From source**), or select from a list of standard units (e.g., inch, foot, millimeter, meter, etc).

7. Depending on the *Import Type,* proceed as follows:

   - If the data is being imported using the **Reference Model** option, there are no additional options that are available. Continue to Step 11.

   - If the data is being imported using the **Convert Model** option, continue to Step 8.

8. (Optional) If you are importing a large data set on a system with limited memory, enable **Reduced Memory Mode**. This option enables you to increase memory capacity, at the cost of performance.

9. In the *Assembly Options* and *Part Options* areas, select how the assembly structure and surfaces are to be imported using the drop-down lists. The options vary depending on the file format being imported as follows:

| File Format | Drop-down List | Options |
|---|---|---|
| **Parts** | • Surfaces | • **Individual:** Surfaces are brought in individually.<br>• **Composite:** A single composite feature. |
| **IGES or STEP files** | • Surfaces | • **Individual:** Surfaces are brought in individually.<br>• **Composite:** A single composite feature.<br>• **Stitch:** Automatically stitches surfaces together on import. |
| **Assemblies** | • Structure<br>• Surfaces | • **Assembly:** The original assembly structure is maintained.<br>• **Multi-body part:** Each component is imported as individual solid bodies in a single part.<br>• **Composite Part:** Each part in an assembly is a composite.<br>• The Part surface options that are available for assemblies are the same as those available for parts. |

10. By default, the name of the newly created file that contains the imported geometry is the same as the imported filename. In the *File Names* area, enter a prefix or suffix to append to the default name in the *Name* field. Additionally, you can browse to a new directory or accept the default file location for the new file.

11. In the *Select* tab, click **Load Model** to add all of the model data to the dialog box and display a preview of the model in the graphics window.

12. (Optional) Click the circular node associated with each node to toggle its inclusion. By default, all nodes are included ( ).

When the node is displayed, the geometry is excluded. To toggle multiple surfaces, select them and use the appropriate Status symbol at the top of the Import dialog box.

- Whether or not you can include or exclude geometry depends on the type of part or assembly that is being imported.

13. (Optional) You can map properties from CATIA, Solidworks, NX, STEP, and Pro-ENGINEER/Creo to standard Autodesk Inventor properties using the **Property Mapping** option. Select the file type that you want to map the Autodesk Inventor properties to fill the values, as required. Click **Save**.

14. Once the options are set, click **OK** to open the imported solid in the Autodesk Inventor software.

> **Hint: Additional Information on Importing CAD Formats**
>
> For more details on the specific formats and versions of other CAD software products that are supported for import, search the Autodesk Inventor Help for "To Import Files from other CAD Systems" or "About Importing Files from other CAD Systems".

# 1.2 Exporting Geometry

To export files, select **Save As>Save Copy As** in the **File** menu. The export file formats that are available for part, assembly, and drawing files are shown in Figure 1–3.

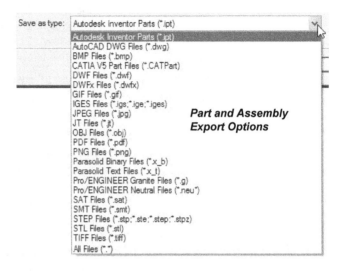

*Part and Assembly Export Options*

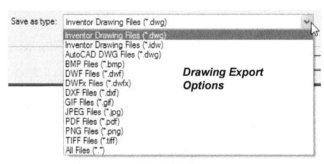

*Drawing Export Options*

**Figure 1–3**

Consider the following when exporting:

- Presentation files can be exported to the following file formats: .DWF, .DWFX, .BMP, .PDF, .PNG, .GIF, .JPG and .TIFF.

- Image files can also be exported by selecting **Export>Image** in the **File** menu.

- Sketches or planar faces can be exported to .DWG or .DXF by right-clicking on a sketch and selecting **Export Sketch As**, or by selecting a planar face, right-clicking on it, and selecting **Export Face As**.

- If you save a file as a .BMP file, a snapshot of the part, assembly, presentation, or drawing file is created as the file displays on the screen.

- SAT files are generally used to translate from a program that uses an ACIS kernel to another. It can also be used to include sketches in the file.

- Sheet metal flat patterns can be exported to .SAT, .DWG, or .DXF formats by right-clicking and selecting **Save Copy As**.

- The .STL file format provides options that enable you to control the facets quality, format, and structure of the file so that an accurate prototype of a part or an assembly file can be sent to a 3D printer.

- The IGES file format enables you to export part geometry and base surfaces and assign them to different layers. Note that only the surfaces visible in the model when exported are included in the exported IGES file.

- Exporting an assembly as a Step file saves all of the files in a single file.

# 1.3 Attaching Point Cloud Data

In addition to the file formats that can be directly opened/imported into the Autodesk Inventor software, you can also attach a point cloud dataset to a new or existing Autodesk Inventor file.

A point cloud file contains a large number of individual vertices that represent the surface of an object(s). The vertices are generally defined with an X, Y, and Z coordinate. The point cloud file is created by a 3D scanning device and can consist of many different file formats. Once imported, the scanned point cloud file can be used to verify fit and function in a top-level assembly file. Figure 1–4 shows an example of a scanned pump system. This piping system could be brought into an assembly model that contains other details of the design.

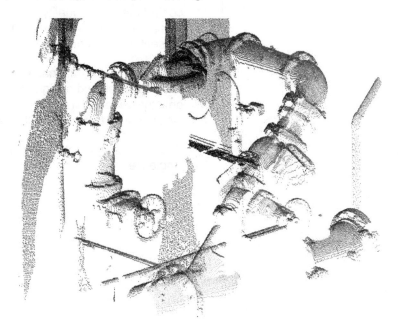

**Figure 1–4**

To attach a point cloud file to an Autodesk Inventor file, it must be first opened in the Autodesk® ReCap software, indexed, and then saved for import into the Autodesk Inventor software.

The point cloud files that can be indexed in the Autodesk® ReCap™ software are shown in Figure 1–5.

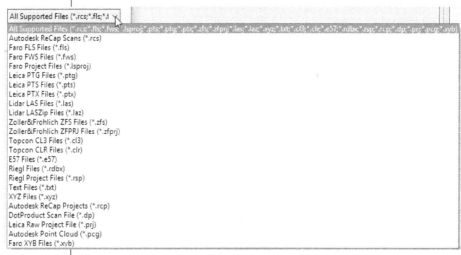

**Figure 1–5**

**Enhanced in 2018**

## How To: Index a Point Cloud File

1. In the *Manage* tab>Point Cloud panel, click (Autodesk ReCap). In the message window that displays, confirm that the Autodesk ReCap software should be launched.
2. Close the Welcome screen.
3. In the top left corner of the interface, select **scan project** to create a new project file to index the point cloud data.
4. Enter a name for the project. A default path for the project is listed below the project name. Select the default path to open the Browse for Folder dialog box and assign a new folder path.
5. Click **proceed** once the project name and folder have been confirmed.
6. On the Import files page, select **select files to import** to open the Import Point Clouds dialog box. Browse to and select a supported point cloud file. Click **Open**.
7. The scan settings become available to clip points (filtering) or define advanced scan options (csys settings, etc.). Define the options, as required.
8. Select **import files** in the lower right-hand corner to begin indexing the data.
9. Once the import has completed, the project is saved in the *Project* directory and the indexed data is saved in the *Project* directory\<project name> folder as an .RCS file.

*Refer to the Autodesk ReCap Help for more information on customizing imported Point Cloud Data.*

10. Select **indexed scans** in the lower right-hand corner to review the list of scanned data.

11. Select **launch project** in the lower right-hand corner to open the project in the Autodesk ReCap software. Once opened, you can use additional tools to manipulate and work with the data.

## How To: Attach a Point Cloud File in a Model

1. In the *Manage* tab>Point Cloud panel, click  (Attach).
2. In the Select Point Cloud File dialog box, select the indexed file (.RCS or .RCP) to attach. Click **Open**.
3. Select a location in the Autodesk Inventor file to place the point cloud data. The Attach Point Cloud dialog box opens enabling you to customize the attachment point and rotation values, and to adjust the density, as shown in Figure 1–6.

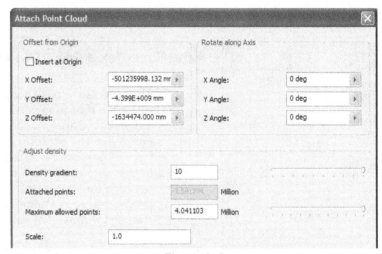

**Figure 1–6**

4. Click **OK** to attach the point cloud. Once imported, the Model browser updates to include a Point Clouds node that lists the imported file, as shown in Figure 1–7.

**Figure 1–7**

Once the point cloud data has been imported, you can use the commands in the Point Cloud panel (as shown in Figure 1–8) to work with the data.

**Figure 1–8**

- Crop the point cloud data to remove unnecessary data from the file. To crop, click ⬚ (Box Crop) in the Point Cloud panel and draw a bounding box around the area that is to be kept. Select an arrow on any of the six sides of the bounding box and drag to change the position of its wall or enter an explicit value, as shown in Figure 1–9. Continue to activate each wall and modify its position as required, to create the required bounding box. Click ✓ to crop.

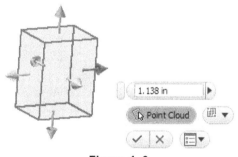

**Figure 1–9**

- Use the **Uncrop** command to remove the previous crop operation and return all of the point cloud data to the file. To uncrop, expand the **Box Crop** command and click ▦ (Uncrop) in the Point Cloud panel.

- Open the Point Cloud Navigator dialog box to control the visibility status of any attached point cloud data. To open the dialog box, click ▨ (Navigator) in the Point Cloud panel and click 💡 next to the data file to toggle its visibility off. Click 💡 to toggle its visibility back on. Its visibility can also be toggled off in the Model browser.

- Add a work point to the model by using a point cloud point as a reference. To create a work point on an existing cloud point, click (Cloud Point) in the Point Cloud panel and select a point. Work points can be used to create additional geometry in the model.

- Add a Work Plane to the model by using points in the point cloud as references. To create a Work Plane, click (Cloud Plane) in the Point Cloud panel and select in the model to create the plane. The plane is inferred from a set of points in the point cloud.

# Practice 1a

# Opening a CATIA Assembly

### Practice Objectives

- Open a CATIA assembly file in Autodesk Inventor by referencing the source data.
- Incorporate changes made to the CATIA model in the Autodesk Inventor model.

In this practice, you open a CATIA assembly file using the **Reference Model** option. By importing the CAD data in this way, changes made in the source model update in the Autodesk Inventor assembly. A change in a CATIA model is made, and you will update the change in the assembly. The final model is shown in Figure 1–10.

**Figure 1–10**

### Task 1 - Import a CATIA assembly file in Autodesk Inventor.

1. In the *Get Started* tab>Launch panel, click ![projects icon] (Projects) to open the Projects dialog box. Project files identify folders that contain the required models.

*This project file is used for the entire training guide.*

2. Click **Browse**. In the *C:\Autodesk Inventor 2018 Working with Imported Data Practice Files* folder, select **Working with Imported Data.ipj**. Click **Open**. The Projects dialog box updates and a check mark displays next to the new project name, indicating that it is the active project. The project file tells Autodesk Inventor where your files are stored. Click **Done**.

3. In the Quick Access Toolbar, click ![open icon].

4. In the Open dialog box, navigate to the *SparkPlug* folder in the practice files folder.

5. In the Files of type drop-down list, select **CATIA V5 Files**.

*Alternatively, the CATIA assembly could be placed in an existing assembly using **Place Imported CAD Files** on the Component panel.*

6. Select **SparkPlug.CATProduct** and click **Open**. The Import dialog box opens.

7. Select **Reference Model** from the *Import Type* area. This assembly is required for use in an Autodesk Inventor assembly model. If changes are made in the source model, the changes must be updated in the Inventor version of the file.

8. In the *Object Filters* area, ensure that only **Solids** is selected. Clear any other options.

9. In the *Inventor Length Units* area, ensure that **From source** is selected. The dialog box updates as shown in Figure 1–11.

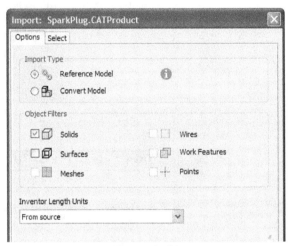

**Figure 1–11**

10. In the *Select* tab, click **Load Model**. A preview of the CATIA assembly displays in the graphics window and the components of the assembly are listed.

11. Click the circular ⊕ node associated with the **Wire.1** component to toggle its status to Excluded (◉). Leave all of the other components as ⊕ Included.

12. Click **OK** to close the dialog box and import the geometry. The assembly is listed in the Model browser, as shown in Figure 1–12.

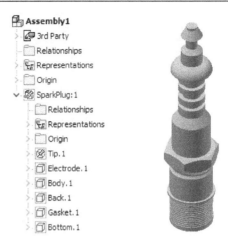

**Figure 1–12**

13. Save the assembly as **Sparkplug.iam** in the *SparkPlug* folder.

## Task 2 - Edit the imported options.

1. In the Model Browser, right-click on **SparkPlug:1** and select **Edit Import** to open the Import dialog box that was used to import the files.

2. In the *Select* tab, select ⬤ adjacent to the **Wire.1** component to include it in the imported geometry.

3. Click **OK** to confirm the change. Note that the component is now listed in the Model browser.

## Task 3 - Edit the imported model geometry.

In this portion of the practice you will simulate making a design change in the original CATIA model. To do this you will rename a file that has been provided to you so that it is used instead of the existing file. This file has had modifications made to it in CATIA. By renaming, you are simulating that the change was made locally to the CATIA file.

1. In Windows Explorer, navigate to your practice files folder and open the *SparkPlug* folder.

2. Select the **Body.CATPart** file and rename it to **Body_OLD.CATPart**.

3. Select the **Body_UPDATED.CATPart** file and rename it to **Body.CATPart**.

4. Return to the Autodesk Inventor software.

5. Note in the Model Browser that the ⚡ icon appears next to the **SparkPlug:1** imported geometry node (it might take a moment to update). In the Quick Access Toolbar, click

   📄 (Local Update) to update the imported geometry with the change that was made in the source model. The model appears as shown in Figure 1–13.

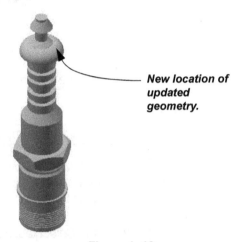

**New location of updated geometry.**

**Figure 1–13**

6. In Model Browser, right-click on **SparkPlug:1** and note the **Suppress Link** and **Break Link** options. These options can be used to either temporarily break the link with the source CATIA model (**Suppress Link**) or permanently break the link (**Break Link**).

7. Save the file and close the window.

# Practice 1b

# Opening STEP Files

### Practice Objectives

- Open a STEP file in the Autodesk Inventor software.
- Edit the imported STEP data to delete a face, move a face, and change its size.
- Add parametric Autodesk Inventor features to the imported geometry.

In this practice, you open auxpart.stp and edit the solid base model to make changes to the imported data. You also add standard Autodesk Inventor features (fillets) to the model and illustrate that the fillet is parametric although the imported geometry is not. The final model is shown in Figure 1–14.

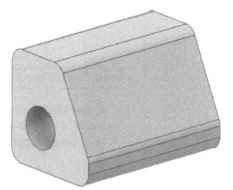

**Figure 1–14**

### Task 1 - Open a part file.

1. In the Quick Access Toolbar, click .

2. In the Open dialog box, in the Files of type drop-down list, select **STEP Files**.

3. Select **auxpart.stp** from the top-level practice files folder. Click **Open**. The Import dialog box opens.

*Step files can also be referenced, if required.*

4. Select **Convert Model** from the *Import Type* area to import the file.

5. In the *Object Filters* area, ensure that **Solids** is selected. Clear any other options, if required.

6. In the *Inventor Length Units* area, ensure that **From source** is selected.

7. In the *Part Options* area, select **Composite** from the Surfaces drop-down list.

8. Click **OK** to close the dialog box and import the geometry. The geometry is listed as **Base1** in the Model browser, as shown in Figure 1–15. The imported solid is a single feature with no associativity between it and the original file.

**Figure 1–15**

---

### Task 2 - Edit the imported model geometry.

---

1. In the Model browser, right-click on **Base1** and select **Edit Solid**. The *Edit Base Solid* tab displays. The panels available provide editing options for imported solids.

2. Select the surface of the hole, as shown in Figure 1–16.

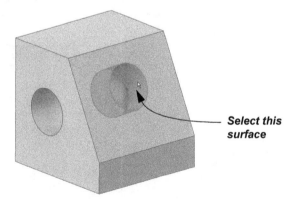

Select this surface

**Figure 1–16**

*The **Move Face** option enables you to select one or more faces on the imported solid to move them in a specified direction.*

3. Right-click and select **Delete** to remove the hole.

4. In the Modify panel, click ⊞ (Move Face). The Move Face mini-toolbar opens.

5. In the mini-toolbar, expand the 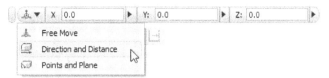 drop-down list and select **Direction and Distance,** as shown in Figure 1–17.

**Figure 1–17**

6. In the mini-toolbar, the **Faces** option is selected by default. Select the hole face as shown in Figure 1–18.

7. In the mini-toolbar, click **Direction** and select the edge indicated in Figure 1–18 to define the direction for the move.

   If required, click to flip the direction of the arrow, as shown in Figure 1–18.

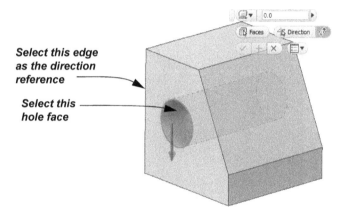

*Select this edge as the direction reference*

*Select this hole face*

**Figure 1–18**

8. In the *Distance* field, enter **0.25**. Complete the move. The part displays as shown in Figure 1–19.

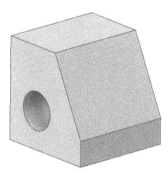

**Figure 1–19**

9. In the Modify panel, click  (Extend/Contract Body). This option resizes an imported solid in a direction perpendicular to a selected plane. The Extend or Contract Body dialog box opens as shown in Figure 1–20.

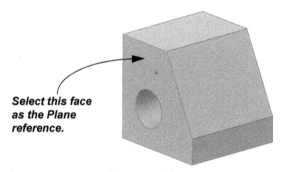

**Figure 1–20**

10. Select the face shown in Figure 1–21 as the reference plane for the extension.

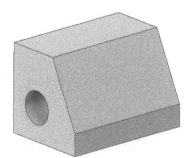

*Select this face as the Plane reference.*

**Figure 1–21**

11. In the *Distance* field, enter **2** and click 🔘 (Expand) to expand the solid part.

12. Click **OK**. The part displays as shown in Figure 1–22. The imported geometry is extended in length by the specified distance.

**Figure 1–22**

13. In the Exit panel, click  (Finish Base Solid).

14. Add fillets to the horizontal edges of the model using the default radius value.

15. In the Model browser, right-click on **Fillet1** and select **Show Dimensions**.

16. Set the new *Radius* to **0.25** and press <Enter>.

17. Update the model to incorporate the dimension change. The part displays as shown in Figure 1–23. Note that the fillet is parametric although the imported geometry is not.

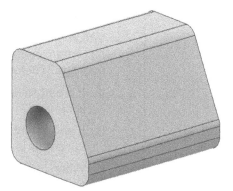

**Figure 1–23**

18. Save the part and close the window.

# Chapter Review Questions

1. CAD data can only be opened into a new Inventor file. CAD data can not be imported into an existing part file.

   a. True

   b. False

2. Which of the following two Import Type opens should be used to ensure that a link to the source file is maintained and that changes that are made to the imported data can be updated.

   a. **Reference Model**

   b. **Convert Model**

3. Which of the statements are true regarding the Import dialog box when importing CAD data from another software package? (Select all that apply.)

   a. If a part file is imported, a new Autodesk Inventor part file is created.

   b. If an assembly is imported, a new Autodesk Inventor assembly is created.

   c. When importing a part into the Autodesk Inventor software, you can set the Part options to recognize each feature as a separate body.

   d. All geometry in the CAD file must be imported. Once imported, you can remove geometry as required.

4. Which of the following menu options enable you to export a .DWG file as a .BMP file? (Select all that apply.)

   a. **File** menu>**Save>Save**

   b. **File** menu>**Save As>Save As**

   c. **File** menu>**Save As>Save Copy As**

   d. **File** menu>**Save As>Save Copy as Template**

   e. **File** menu>**Export>Image**

5. Which software product should you use to index the point cloud data before importing it into the Autodesk Inventor software?

a. Autodesk® Revit®

b. Autodesk® Inventor®

c. Autodesk® ReCap™

d. Autodesk® Alias®

# Command Summary

| Button | Command | Location |
|---|---|---|
| | **Autodesk ReCap** | • **Ribbon:** *Manage* tab>Point Cloud panel |
| NA | **Export Face As** | • **Browser:** right-click a face |
| | **Export Image** | • **File menu:** Export |
| NA | **Export Sketch As** | • **Browser:** right-click a sketch |
| | **Import** | • **Ribbon:** *3D Model* tab>Create panel<br>• **Ribbon:** *Manage* tab>Import panel<br>• **Ribbon:** *Assemble* tab>expanded Place commands |
| | **Open** | • **Ribbon:** *Get Started* tab>Launch panel<br>• **Quick Access toolbar**<br>• **File menu** |
| | **Save Copy As** | • **File menu:** Save As |

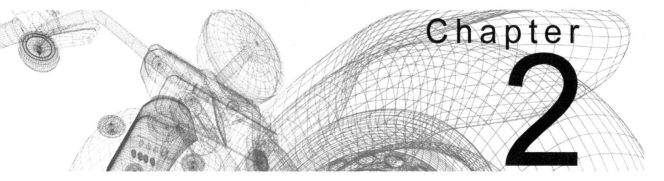

# Chapter 2

# Working with Imported Solids

The Autodesk® Inventor® software supports the import of files from many different types of 3D CAD programs. In some cases, an associative link can be maintained between the source file and the Autodesk Inventor software. Once a CAD file has been imported, the geometry is brought into an Autodesk Inventor file where it can be further manipulated using tools available in the software. Understanding the editing tools that are available to further manipulate the imported geometry is essential to ensuring the efficient creation of the required model.

## Learning Objectives in this Chapter

- Use the Edit Base Solid environment to edit solids that have been imported into the Autodesk Inventor software.
- Create Direct Edit features in a model that move, resize, scale, rotate, and delete existing geometry in both imported and native Autodesk Inventor files.

# 2.1 Editing the Base Solid

To edit a solid base feature that has been imported, right-click on the base feature in the Model browser and select **Edit Solid**. The *Edit Base Solid* tab displays, as shown in Figure 2–1, providing the editing options for imported solids.

Figure 2–1

## Move Face

The 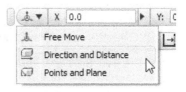 (Move Face) options enable you to select faces to be moved. There are three move options in the mini-toolbar

drop-down list - **Free Move**, **Direction and Distance**, and **Points and Plane**, as shown in Figure 2–2.

Figure 2–2

Figure 2–3 shows the mini-toolbar for the **Free Move** option. The hole face can be dragged or assigned to an X, Y, Z location.

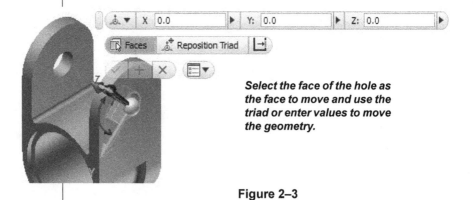

*Select the face of the hole as the face to move and use the triad or enter values to move the geometry.*

Figure 2–3

Figure 2–4 displays the mini-toolbar for the **Direction and Distance** option. The hole face can be moved relative to the selected distance reference.

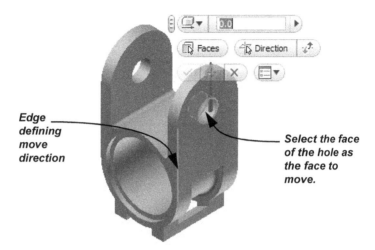

*Edge defining move direction*

*Select the face of the hole as the face to move.*

**Figure 2–4**

Figure 2–5 displays the mini-toolbar for the **Points and Plane** option. The hole face can be moved to a selected point.

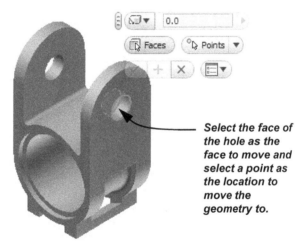

*Select the face of the hole as the face to move and select a point as the location to move the geometry to.*

**Figure 2–5**

## Offset

The 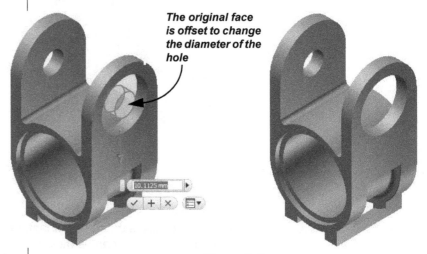 (Offset) option enables you to offset the existing face by a specified value or by dynamically pressing and pulling the face, as required. The face shown on the left in Figure 2–6 is selected and offset to change its diameter.

*The original face is offset to change the diameter of the hole*

**Figure 2–6**

## Extend or Contract Body

The (Extend/Contract Body) option enables you to resize an imported solid in a direction perpendicular to a selected plane. In Figure 2–7, a plane was selected at the bottom of the part as the reference for an extension. The imported geometry is extended by the specified distance.

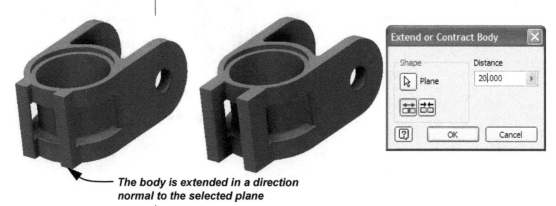

*The body is extended in a direction normal to the selected plane*

**Figure 2–7**

## Delete Faces

To delete faces from the imported solid, select the faces and select **Delete** in the shortcut menu. In Figure 2–8, a face is selected and deleted from the imported solid. The geometry updates to account for the deleted face.

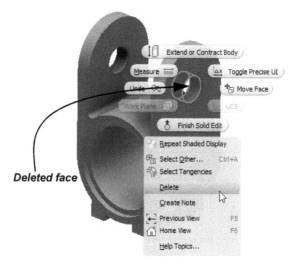

Figure 2–8

## 2.2 Direct Edit

Direct Edit is a method of editing both imported data and native Autodesk Inventor parametric models. These tools enable you to delete and adjust the size, scale, shape, and location of features by directly manipulating geometry in the model.

Uses of Direct Edit include:

- Incorporating quick yet precise changes to parametric data without changing the initial feature settings. The edits can still be considered parametric because they are added to the Model browser and can be edited.

- Making changes to imported Base Solid data.

To start the **Direct Edit** command, in the *3D Model* tab>Modify panel, click  (Direct). Alternatively, you can right-click on imported geometry in the Model browser and select **Direct Edit**. The Direct Edit mini-toolbar opens, which provides access to all of the Direct Edit tools, as shown in Figure 2–9. These tools are activated in the top row of the mini-toolbar and the remaining tools in the mini-toolbar update to support the selected editing type.

**Figure 2–9**

## Move

### How To: Move Geometry

1. In the mini-toolbar, click **Move**. The tools in the mini-toolbar update to permit the moving of the geometry, as shown in Figure 2–10.
2. Use the Geometry Type drop-down list to select the geometry type that is going to be selected for moving. The options include faces and solids. Select the geometry in the model that you want to move. A triad displays on the model to define the move direction, as shown in Figure 2–10.

**Figure 2–10**

3. The triad location in the model displays based on the location where the selection was made (identified with a green dot). The commands on the second line of the mini-toolbar enable you to manipulate the triad's location:

- Click **Locate** to select a new location on the selected face. Hover the cursor over the selected face until the required placement location is highlighted in green and select to move it.

- Click **Locate** or **World** to reorient the direction of triad axis based on the selected object (local) or the model origin (world), respectively.

- When a local system is used, click  to realign the triad to other geometry in the model.

4. Select the arrow head on the appropriate triad axis to move the selected face or solid in that direction. To define the move with more accuracy, use either of the following:

- Click **Measure From** to specify a start point and display an *Offset* field to accurately enter an offset value. In the example shown in Figure 2–11, the midpoint on the back edge was selected as a measurement reference and a value was entered.

*The midpoint of this edge was selected as a reference point from which to measure.*

**Figure 2–11**

- Click **Snap To** to select a specific reference point on the geometry to which to move.

5. Click  to apply the operation. ⏴ displays on the model indicating a **Move** operation was added to the Direct Edit feature. The Model browser also updates to indicate that a **Move** operation was added, as shown in Figure 2–12.

> Extrusion 10
> Extrusion 11
> ∨ Direct Edit 1
>     Move 1
>     End of Part

**Figure 2–12**

6. Continue to incorporate other direct edit manipulations in the model or click ⓧ to close the **Direct Edit** command.

## Size

### How To: Resize Geometry

1. In the mini-toolbar, click **Size**. The tools in the mini-toolbar update to permit the resizing of geometry, as shown in Figure 2–13.

**Figure 2–13**

2. Select a face(s) in the model to resize it.
3. Drag the arrow or enter a value in the value field to define the new size. The face shown in Figure 2–14 is being resized.

**Figure 2–14**

4. Depending on the selected reference, the Modifier drop-down list shown in Figure 2–15 provides control over how the selected face is resized. For example, **Offset** enables you to enter a distance value, **Diameter** is used to change the size of cylindrical faces, and **Radius** changes the size of radial faces.

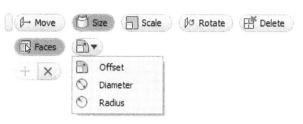

**Figure 2–15**

5. Click  to apply the operation. displays on the model indicating that resizing was done to the face and added to the Direct Edit feature. The Model browser also updates to indicate that a **Size** operation was added to the Direct Edit feature, as shown in Figure 2–16.

**Figure 2–16**

6. Continue to incorporate other direct edit manipulations to the model or click ✕ to close the **Direct Edit** command.

## Scale

### How To: Scale Geometry

1. In the mini-toolbar, click **Scale**. The tools in the mini-toolbar update to permit the scaling of geometry, as shown in Figure 2–17.

**Figure 2–17**

2. Select the solid that you want to scale.

3. In the drop-down list on the third line of the mini-toolbar select whether the scaling will be **Uniform** or **Non Uniform**.

4. The triad location appears at a system-defined location on the model. The commands on the second line of the mini-toolbar enable you to manipulate the triad's location:

   • Click **Locate** to select a new location on the selected face. Hover the cursor over the selected face until an acceptable placement location is highlighted in green and select to move it.

   • Click **Local** or **World** to reorient the direction of the triad axis based on the selected object (local) or the model origin (world), respectively. This option is only available if the scaling is set to **Non Uniform**.

   • When a local system is used, click 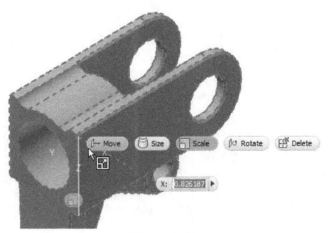 to realign the triad to other geometry in the model. This option is only available if the scaling is set to **Non Uniform**.

5. Drag the arrow or enter a value in the value field(s) to define the scaling value. For a non-uniform scaling, you can enter values in all three directions. Figure 2–18 shows uniform scaling.

**Figure 2–18**

6. Click  to apply the operation. ⬚ displays on the model indicating that a scaling operation was added to the Direct Edit feature. The Model browser also updates to indicate that a **Scale** operation was added to the Direct Edit feature, as shown in Figure 2–19.

> ⊔⌶ Extrusion10
> ⬚↑ Extrusion11
⌄ ◨ Direct Edit3
⬚ Scale1
◯ End of Part

**Figure 2–19**

7. Continue to incorporate other direct edit manipulations to the model, or click ✕ to close the **Direct Edit** command.

## Rotate

## How To: Rotate Geometry

1. In the mini-toolbar, click **Rotate**. The tools in the mini-toolbar update to permit the rotation of geometry, as shown in Figure 2–20.

**Figure 2–20**

2. Use the Geometry Type drop-down list to select the geometry type that is going to be selected for rotating. The options include faces and solids. Select the geometry in the model that you want to rotate. A triad displays on the model to define the rotate direction, as shown in Figure 2–21.

**Figure 2–21**

3. The triad location in the model displays based on the location on the face or solid at which you select the geometry (identified with green dot). The commands on the second line of the mini-toolbar enable you to manipulate the triad's location:

- Click **Locate** to select a new location on the selected face. Hover the cursor over the selected face until an acceptable placement location is highlighted in green and select to move it.

- Click **Local** or **World** to reorient the direction of the triad axis based on the selected object (local) or the model origin (world), respectively.

- When a local system is used, click 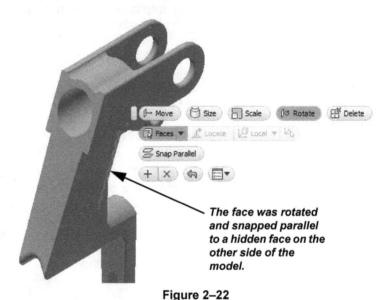 to realign the triad to other geometry in the model.

4. Select the rotation wheel on the appropriate triad axis to rotate the selected face or solid in that direction. To define the rotation with more accuracy, click **Snap Parallel** to specify another plane to which the selected face should be set parallel, as shown in Figure 2–22.

*The face was rotated and snapped parallel to a hidden face on the other side of the model.*

Figure 2–22

5. Click to apply the operation. displays on the model indicating that a **Rotation** operation was added to the Direct Edit feature. The Model browser also updates to indicate that a **Rotation** operation was added to the Direct Edit feature, as shown in Figure 2–23.

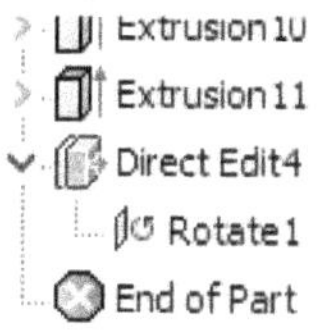

Extrusion10
Extrusion11
Direct Edit4
Rotate1
End of Part

**Figure 2–23**

6. Continue to incorporate other direct edit manipulations to the model or click to close the **Direct Edit** command.

## Delete

### How To: Delete Geometry

1. In the mini-toolbar, click **Delete**. The tools in the mini-toolbar update to permit the deleting of geometry, as shown in Figure 2–24.

Move
Size
Scale
Rotate
Delete
Faces

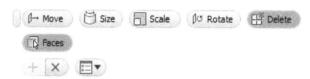

**Figure 2–24**

2. Select a face in the model to delete it.
3. Click to apply the operation. displays on the model indicating that a deletion was made in the model. The Model browser also updates to indicate that a **Delete** operation was added to the Direct Edit feature, as shown in Figure 2–25.

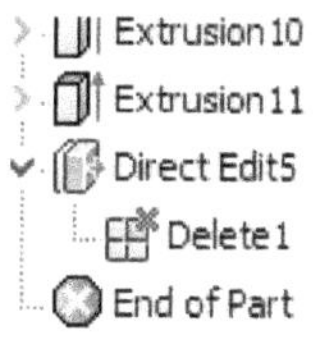

Extrusion10
Extrusion11
Direct Edit5
Delete1
End of Part

**Figure 2–25**

4. Continue to incorporate other direct edit manipulations to the model or click to close the **Direct Edit** command.

## Hint: Direct Edit Operation Failures

When adding a **Direct Edit** operation, 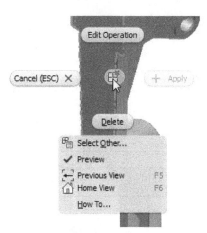 might display in the mini-toolbar after the reference has been selected. It indicates that the operation cannot be done on this reference. For example, surfaces can only be deleted if the geometry still forms a solid after deletion. The face generated from the hole geometry can be deleted, but an outside face of the model cannot. To delete an outside face, consider using the **Delete Face** command in the Modify panel. This command coverts the model to a surface model once an outside face is deleted.

To undo a failed face selection, click (Reset) to reset the operation or hold <Ctrl> and select the failing face again to remove it from the selection.

Once changes have been made with **Direct Edit** you can decide whether to edit, delete, or apply the edits to the parametric feature history (if available). This is done while the Direct Edit feature is active by right-clicking on the operation symbol that was added to the model, as shown in Figure 2–26.

Edit Operation

Cancel (ESC) ✕          ＋ Apply

Delete

- Select Other...
- ✓ Preview
- ← Previous View          F5
- ⌂ Home View          F6
- How To...

**Figure 2–26**

# Practice 2a

# Direct Edit

## Practice Objectives

- Open a CATIA part model and review the base solid geometry that was imported.
- Edit the base solid geometry using the Direct Edit option to move, resize, rotate, and delete faces on imported geometry.

In this practice you will learn how to use the **Direct Edit** option to edit base solid geometry that was imported into the Autodesk Inventor software. Faces will be deleted, moved, resized, and rotated to obtain the required modified geometry. To complete the practice you are also provided with a native Autodesk Inventor file to edit using the Direct Edit tools.

## Task 1 - Open a CATIA model.

1. Open the **Cover.CATPart** model from the practice files folder. The Import dialog box opens.

2. In the *Import Type* area, select **Convert Model** to import the geometry and break the link with the original model.

3. In the *Object Filters* area, ensure that **Solids** is selected. Clear any other options, if required.

4. In the *Inventor Length Units* area, ensure that **From source** is selected.

5. In the *Part Options* area, select **Composite** from the Surfaces drop-down list.

6. Click **OK** to close the dialog box and import the geometry. The Model browser shows that a base feature called Casting has been imported, as shown in Figure 2–27.

**Figure 2–27**

### Task 2 - Edit the Base Solid that was imported to move a face.

1. In the *3D Model* tab>Modify panel, click  (Direct). The Direct Edit mini-toolbar opens, as shown in Figure 2–28.

**Figure 2–28**

2. Ensure that **Move** is selected in the mini-toolbar. Hover the cursor over the face shown in Figure 2–29 as the face to be moved. Hold <Ctrl> to maintain this surface while locating the control point. Hover the cursor over different vertices on the face before selecting. The highlighted green dot determines where the triad will be located for moving. Ensure that you select in the area shown to place the triad and begin moving the face.

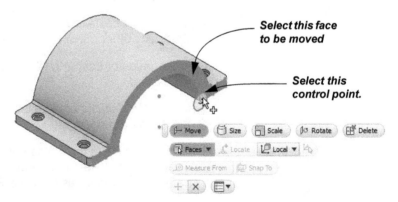

Select this face to be moved

Select this control point.

**Figure 2–29**

3. By default, the x-axis (local to the model) is active. As indicated by the gold colored x-axis on the triad. Drag the face outward by dragging the arrowhead, as shown in Figure 2–30.

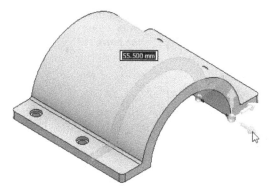

**Figure 2–30**

4. Enter **50** as the value by which the face will be moved and click ⊞ to complete the **Move** operation.

5. Note that ⊢ displays on the model, indicating that the move exists in the Direct Edit feature, as shown in Figure 2–31. **Move1** also displays in the Model browser in the Direct Edit feature.

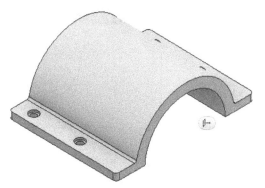

**Figure 2–31**

6. Right-click on ⊢ and select **Edit Operation** to edit the **Move** operation that was just added.

7. Instead of entering a specific value to move the face, the required depth is to be measured relative to the back surface. Click **Measure From** and select the edge shown in Figure 2–32. Enter **180** as the value.

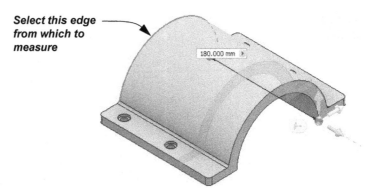

*Select this edge from which to measure*

Figure 2–32

8. Click ⊕ to complete the changes.

9. Select the face shown in Figure 2–33 and move it **20mm**. Do the same on the opposite face. Once the two **Move** operations have been added the model displays as shown in Figure 2–33.

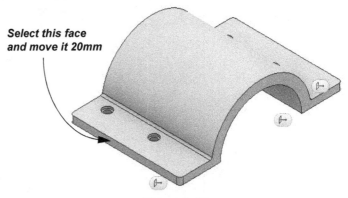

*Select this face and move it 20mm*

Figure 2–33

## Task 3 - Edit the position and size of the holes.

1. In the mini-toolbar, select **Delete** to activate the **Delete** operation.

2. Select the four faces that were created in the holes as counterbores. Two of these faces are shown in Figure 2–34, but select all four.

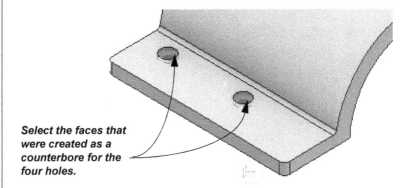

**Select the faces that were created as a counterbore for the four holes.**

**Figure 2–34**

3. Click ⊕ to complete the operation. Four operations have now been added to the Direct Edit feature.

4. Click **Size** and select the surface of the hole shown in Figure 2–35.

5. Drag the triad arrow head. Enter **-6** to enlarge the diameter by an exact value, as shown in Figure 2–35.

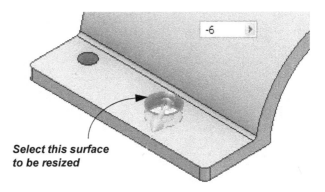

**Select this surface to be resized**

**Figure 2–35**

6. Click ⊕ to complete the operation.

7. With **Size** still active, select the inside face of the hole that you just resized.

8. Expand 🗂▼ and select **Diameter**.

9. Select the hole faces in the three remaining holes, as shown in Figure 2–36. This sets the size of the three selected faces to that of the previously modified hole.

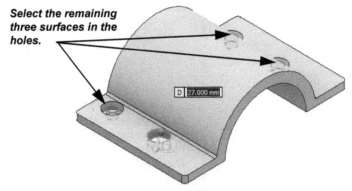

*Select the remaining three surfaces in the holes.*

**Figure 2–36**

10. Click 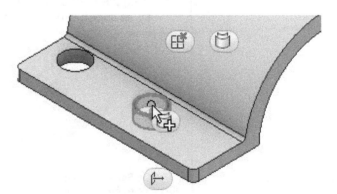 to complete the operation.

11. Click **Move** and select the surface of the hole shown in Figure 2–37. Ensure that the highlighted green point is at the center of the circle to enable you to move the center of the hole.

**Figure 2–37**

12. Ensure the x-axis arrow on the triad is selected.

13. Click **Measure From** and select the front edge (midpoint) of the model, as shown in Figure 2–38. Enter **-25mm** as the value. Do not press <Enter>.

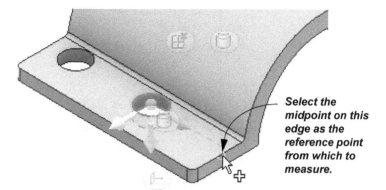

*Select the midpoint on this edge as the reference point from which to measure.*

**Figure 2–38**

14. Select the y-axis arrow on the triad.

15. Click **Measure From** and select the side edge as shown in Figure 2–39. Enter **-25mm** as the value and press <Enter> to complete the operation.

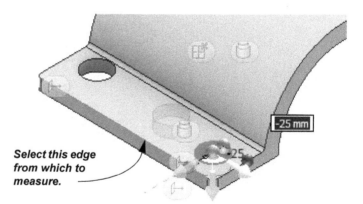

*Select this edge from which to measure.*

**Figure 2–39**

16. Adjust the positions of the other three holes in the model so that they are positioned in the same way from their nearest edges. The model should display similar to shown in Figure 2–40.

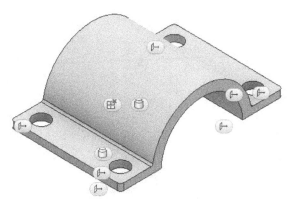

**Figure 2–40**

## Task 4 - Rotate faces and scale the model.

1. Click **Rotate** and hover the cursor over the surface shown in Figure 2–41. Holding <Ctrl>, continue to move the mouse and ensure that the highlighted green point is at the center of the edge shown. Press the left mouse button to select it. You are now able to rotate as required from this point.

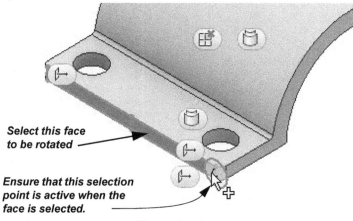

*Select this face to be rotated*

*Ensure that this selection point is active when the face is selected.*

**Figure 2–41**

2. Rotate the wheel as shown in Figure 2–42. Drag the triad to **20.00 deg**. Alternatively, you can enter the value. Press <Enter>.

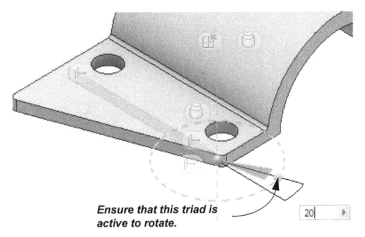

*Ensure that this triad is active to rotate.*

**Figure 2–42**

3. Rotate the opposite edge in the same way. Review the Model browser and note that all of the operations are listed in the Direct Edit feature.

4. Click ⊠ to cancel the Direct Edit feature. The model displays as shown in Figure 2–43.

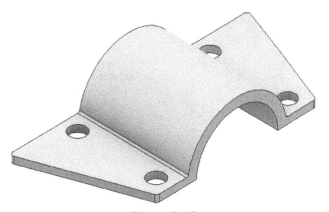

**Figure 2–43**

5. Note that the Model browser lists the Direct Edit feature and that the operations are no longer displayed. To edit or review the operations you must edit the feature.

6.  Double-click on the **Direct Edit** feature in the Model browser.

7.  Right-click on 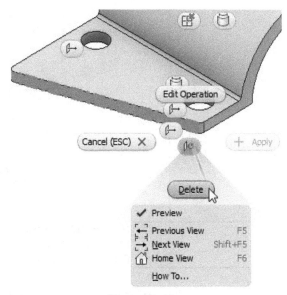 in the graphics window and select **Delete** (as shown in Figure 2–44), to remove the operation from the model.

**Figure 2–44**

8.  Remove the second **Rotate** operation.

9.  Click **Scale** and select the solid body shown in Figure 2–45.

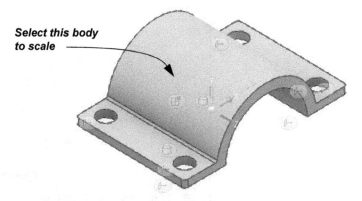

*Select this body to scale*

**Figure 2–45**

10. Ensure that the X axis manipulator is active. Enter **2** in the entry field and press <Enter> to scale the model.

11. Click ☒ to cancel the Direct Edit feature.

12. Save the model and close the window.

---

**Hint: Using Direct Edit with Referenced CAD models.**

It is not recommended to add Direct Edit features to a CAD model that has been imported and maintains its link to the source CAD model. This is because the Direct Edit feature may fail if the model changes in the source CAD tool.

---

# Chapter Review Questions

1. Which commands can be used to edit the Base geometry shown on the left in Figure 2–46 to create the geometry shown on the right in Figure 2–46? (Select all that apply.)

 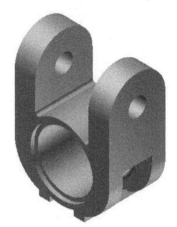

Figure 2–46

   a. Move Face

   b. Offset

   c. Extend/Contract Body

   d. Delete

2. The **Extend/Contract Body** option in the Edit Base Solid ribbon enables you to resize selected features on an import solid.

   a. True

   b. False

3. How many **Delete** operations were completed on the model on the left side in Figure 2–47 to obtain the model shown on the right side in Figure 2–47?

 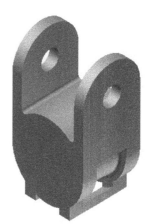

**Figure 2–47**

a. 1

b. 2

c. 4

d. None, delete would not obtain this final geometry.

4. Which of the following are Direct Edit tools that are available in the Direct Edit mini-toolbar? (Select all that apply.)

a. **Move**

b. **Size**

c. **Define Envelopes**

d. **Rotate**

e. **Remove Details**

f. **Delete**

g. **Scale**

5. The green dot that is highlighted on a face that is being relocated using the **Direct Edit** command indicates where the triad is placed.

a. True

b. False

6. Which of the following enables you to define the measurement reference point when using **Direct Edit**?

   a. **Measure From**

   b. **Snap To**

   c.

   d. **Snap Parallel**

7. Which of the following icons displays in the Direct Edit mini-toolbar when a face in the exterior geometry on the model is selected for deletion?

   a.

   b.

   c.

   d.

# Command Summary

| Button | Command | Location |
|--------|---------|----------|
| N/A | **Delete Face** | • **Context menu:** In graphics window |
| | **Direct Edit** | • **Ribbon:** *3D Model* tab>Modify panel<br>• **Context menu:** In graphics window |
| | **Extend/ Contract Body** | • **Ribbon:** *Edit Base Solid* tab>Modify panel |
| | **Move Face** | • **Ribbon:** *Edit Base Solid* tab>Modify panel |
| | **Offset** | • **Ribbon:** *Edit Base Solid* tab>Modify panel |

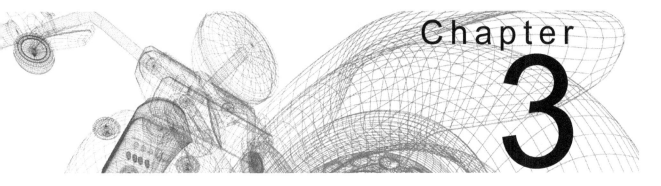

# Chapter 3

# Working with Imported Surfaces

The data that is imported from other CAD systems may have errors that prevents it from being created as a solid in Autodesk® Inventor®. Additionally, surfaces that are imported may need to be individually selected for modification to make a required design change. Situations like these require you to fix the problem areas or finish surface modeling. There are many options that can be used to help you identify and fix these errors.

## Learning Objectives in this Chapter

- Set the import options to import surface data from other file format types.
- Transfer imported surface data into the Repair Environment to conduct a quality check for errors.
- Appropriately set the stitch tolerance value so that gaps in the imported geometry can be automatically stitched and identify the gaps that are not stitched.
- Use the Repair Environment commands to repair gaps or delete, extend, replace, trim and break surfaces to successfully create a solid from the imported geometry.

# 3.1 Importing Surfaces

As previously discussed, the Import dialog box can be used to import many different CAD file formats. In addition to this, it also has the flexibility to only import surface data from a file. Once the surface data is imported, you can manipulate it using the standard surfacing tools to create required geometry or edit existing surface geometry. The workflow is similar, however you should consider the following:

- Ensure that the selected **Import Type** option captures your design intent, so that the model is either referenced or converted for use in Autodesk Inventor.

- In the *Object Filter* area, select the **Surface** option to provide you with the required surfaces.

- Consider using the *Select* tab to selectively include or exclude surfaces that are to be imported, if available. For example, when importing an .IGS file, you can select the specific surfaces to import, as shown in Figure 3–1.

**Figure 3–1**

## How To: Include or Exclude Surfaces

1. Select the *Select* tab.
2. Select **Load Model** to add all of the model data to the dialog box and display a preview of the model in the graphics window.
3. Click the circular node associated with each surface to toggle its inclusion. By default, all surfaces are included ( ). When the node is displayed, the surface is excluded. To toggle multiple surfaces, select them and use the appropriate Status symbol at the top of the Import dialog box.

# 3.2 Repairing Imported Surfaces

When you import surfaces, the data might have to be repaired and stitched together into a quilt (a group of surfaces), before the surfaces can be used. Alternatively, you simply might want to make design changes to the geometry. To accomplish this, you should use the Repair environment. In the Repair environment, you can analyze, repair, and stitch the surfaces. You can then return to the Part environment to repair any remaining problem areas, such as creating missing surfaces, and finally stitching the surfaces together. If the surfaces you stitch form a closed boundary, you can obtain a solid geometry.

**General Steps**

Use the following general steps to repair imported surfaces:

1. Switch to the Repair environment.
2. Perform an error check.
3. Stitch surfaces together.
4. Repair imported surfaces.
5. Stitch surfaces together, as required.
6. Perform an error check.
7. Complete the repair.
8. Repair remaining problem areas, as required.
9. Stitch surfaces together, as required.

## Step 1 - Switch to the Repair environment.

To access the Repair environment, right-click on the imported geometry node and select **Repair Bodies**. Alternatively, in the Surface panel, you can click  (Repair Bodies) and then select the body to be repaired.

The *Repair* tab displays as shown in Figure 3–2.

**Figure 3–2**

## Step 2 - Perform an error check.

Perform an error check to check for surface topology, geometry, and modeling uncertainty errors. In the Repair panel, click

(Find Errors). Alternatively, you can right-click on the repair node or in the graphics window and select **Find Errors.** The Find Errors dialog box opens. Click **Select All** to select all the bodies in the imported geometry or manually select bodies. Click **OK** to run the check. The check analyzes the imported data and reports the errors, by type, in the Model browser. The error type is identified by the following symbols:

- The ✔ symbol identifies healthy geometry in the model.

- The ⓘ symbol identifies geometry that needs further investigation.

- The ⚠ symbol identifies geometry that contains errors and requires repairing.

*A glyph for each error can be displayed on the model. Right-click on the error folder and select **Error Glyph Visibility**.*

Similar errors are all grouped into folders. To locate an error in the model, in the Model browser select the error and the error symbol. Its associated entity is highlighted in the model and an error glyph is displayed. Additionally, you can use the

⇐ (Previous Error) and ⇒ (Next Error) options to progress through the list.

### Heal Errors

*Refer to the Help documentation for a complete list and description of the possible error types that can be found.*

The **Heal Errors** command can also be used in the Repair panel

when errors exist. Click (Heal Errors), select the bodies that are required to be healed, and enter a healing tolerance value.

With the required bodies selected, you can click (Analyze Selected Bodies) to analyze if the assigned tolerance will resolve the issues. Click **OK** to run the healing process. The bodies are analyzed and any problems are reported. Errors that can be healed are corrected in the model, otherwise continue to use the options in the Modify panel to correct the geometry.

### Repairing using the mini-toolbar

Not all errors can be resolved using the **Heal Errors** command. As each error is selected, a Repair mini-toolbar is displayed to help resolve the error. The resolution options that are available are dependent on the error. For example, you may be provided tools to delete faces, create patches or stitch the geometry. Click

 once the error is healed.

## Step 3 - Stitch surfaces together.

Perform a stitch to close any insignificant gaps that might have resulted from the import. It also helps to locate the significant gaps and over-extended surfaces. Stitch creates a quilt of the stitched surfaces. It is better to initially use a smaller tolerance to avoid undesirable changes in the geometry and then increase the tolerance, as required. When a gap or overlap exists that is too large to stitch without affecting the integrity of the surfaces, use the other surface repair options available.

### How To: Stitch the Surfaces

1. In the Modify panel, click ▤ (Stitch) or right-click in the graphics window and select **Stitch**.
2. In the Select area of the dialog box, define whether the entities to be stitched are to be selected as faces or bodies. The faces or bodies can be selected in the Model browser or directly on the model. To select all entities in the model, select and drag a bounding box around the model. The Stitch dialog box updates showing the number of faces selected.
3. Enter a value in the *Fill gaps smaller than* field. This maximum tolerance value identifies the maximum gap and overlap between two surfaces that will be stitched together. Surface edges that contain a gap or overlap less than the maximum tolerance are stitched.

4. To preview a list of edges that will not be stitched, click

(Find remaining gaps and free edges). Edges that could not be stitched (due to them being further apart than the defined maximum tolerance) are highlighted in the model and listed in the Stitch dialog box. An example of a model that is stitched but still contains free edges is shown in Figure 3–3.

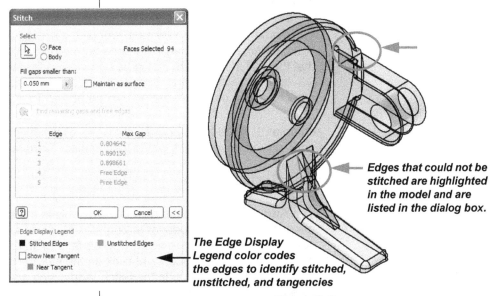

*Edges that could not be stitched are highlighted in the model and are listed in the dialog box.*

*The Edge Display Legend color codes the edges to identify stitched, unstitched, and tangencies*

**Figure 3–3**

5. To determine which edge in the model corresponds to which edge listed in the dialog box, select a row in the list. The corresponding edge highlights in the model. Some of the edge gaps and overlaps might be small so you might need to zoom in to see them.

6. Review the list of gaps or overlaps. If they are insignificant and can be repaired by adjusting the tolerance value without adversely affecting surrounding surfaces, change the tolerance and click **OK**. If not, maintain the original tolerance and click **OK**. Plan to use the tools on the Modify panel to fix the model.

## Step 4 - Repair imported surfaces.

Use the following options in the Modify panel of the Repair environment or in the right-click on the marking or context menu to repair the imported surfaces.

### Transfer Surface

The **Transfer Surface** command works in a similar way to the Stitch command. The only difference between the commands is that the Transfer Surface dialog box provides a field that enables you to select a destination body to move the selected face or body to or you can generate a new composite. To access the command, in the Modify panel, click ![icon] (Transfer Surface) or right-click in the graphics window and select **Transfer Surface**.

### Add Surface

The **Add Surface** command is only available in the shortcut menu directly in the model or through the Model browser. The command can be used to add a new surface to an existing face or body. To add a surface, right-click on the surface to be added and select **Add Surface**. In the Stitch: Add dialog box, select the face/body to which the new surface will be added, enter the gap tolerance value, and click **OK**.

### Unstitch

There are times when you need to select particular surfaces in a quilt. Unless the required surface is unstitched from the quilt, you cannot select it. To unstitch, click ![icon] (Unstitch), select the surface(s) to exclude from the quilt, and click **Apply**. You can also access the **Unstitch** command by right-clicking in the graphics window. The unstitched surface(s) can then be selected separately from the rest of the quilt.

### Extend Faces

*To select a reference to which a surface can extend up to (instead of having to specify a distance), use **Extend Surface** in the Part Features Panel.*

Use Extend Faces to extend faces at an edge, as shown in Figure 3–4. To extend a face, click ![icon] (Extend Faces), select the edge reference(s) for the extend, enter the extension distance, and click **Apply**. The face is extended by the specified distance.

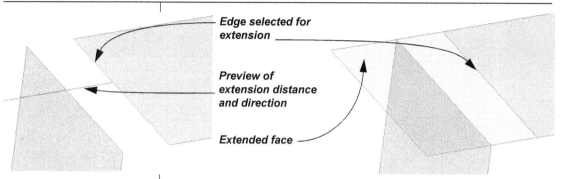

*Edge selected for extension*

*Preview of extension distance and direction*

*Extended face*

**Figure 3–4**

## Intersect Faces

Use Intersect Faces to trim or break faces that intersect one another, as shown in Figure 3–5. To trim faces, click

⬛ (Intersect Faces), click ⬛ (Trim), and select the portions of the faces to keep when selecting the faces for the trim. The portions of the faces you did not select are removed starting at

the line of intersection. To break faces, click ⬛ (Intersect

Faces), click ⬛ (Break), and select the faces for the break. The faces are broken in two at the line of intersection.

*Initial surfaces*

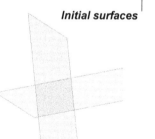

*Portions of the surfaces are removed after the trim*

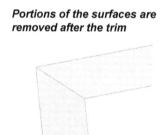

*Four surfaces exist after the break*

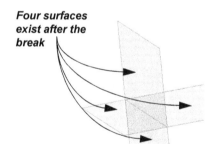

**Figure 3–5**

## Edit Regions

Edit Regions removes unnecessary regions and loops (e.g., a surface containing a hole that needs to be removed or a self-intersecting loop needs to be removed). To edit regions, click

⬛ (Edit Regions), select a face to repair, select regions in the face to keep, and click **Done**. The regions you selected are retained and the regions and unnecessary loops are removed.

## Extract Loop and Boundary Trim

During IGES or STEP surface data translation, faces can be trimmed unexpectedly. Use **Extract Loop** to untrim surfaces and then use **Boundary Trim** to trim the surfaces using the required boundary.

To extract loop, click ▣ (Extract Loop), select one or more loops from one surface, select **Delete Wires** to delete the original loop on the surface, and click **Apply**. Click **Done** if no additional extractions are required. An example of a loop that was extracted is shown in Figure 3–6.

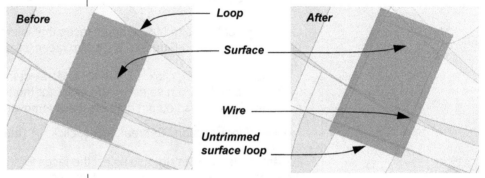

**Figure 3–6**

To trim a boundary, click 🗞 (Boundary Trim) and select edges that form a closed loop. Once the loop is closed, select the side of the face to keep or the loop to replace. An example is shown in Figure 3–7.

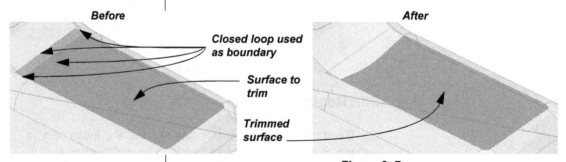

**Figure 3–7**

*Boundary Patches can be created both in the repair and part environments.*

## Boundary Patch

Boundary Patch enables you to create a surface from closed boundary edges. To create a Boundary Patch, click

(Boundary Patch), and select a closed 2D or 3D sketch, or select edges from existing objects to form a closed profile. Click **OK** to create the surface. A planar patch surface created from a closed 2D sketch is shown in Figure 3–8.

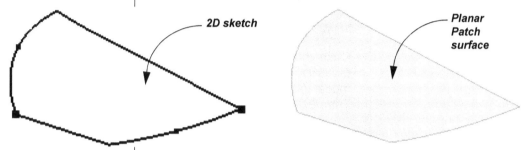

Figure 3–8

## Reverse Normal

The **Reverse Normal** option enables you to toggle the direction of the surface normal for a face or a lump. Once you select a reference, the surface is highlighted in green and shows the default normal direction with an arrow. This is only available while in the Repair environment.

### Step 5 - Stitch surfaces together, as required.

Stitch any additional surfaces you created together, as required. If the stitched surfaces form an enclosed boundary, it will be indicated in the Model browser as a Solid surface.

### Step 6 - Perform an error check.

Perform an additional error check to verify the validity of the surfaces. If issues still remain, use any of the repair options to resolve the issues.

## Step 7 - Complete the repair.

Once you have finished working in the Repair environment, you can right-click in the graphics window and select **Finish Repair** or in the Exit panel, click  (Finish Repair).

## Step 8 - Repair remaining problem areas, as required.

Once you have left the Repair environment you are placed in the Modeling environment. You can continue to interact with your model using the standard *3D Model* tab options (e.g., Patch, Trim, Extend) to further resolve any problem areas.

## Step 9 - Stitch surfaces together, as required.

Stitch the additional surfaces that were created or modified, as required. If the stitched surfaces form a fully enclosed boundary (and assuming that no other solid bodies exist in the part) the quilt generates a solid base feature in the part.

# Practice 3a

# Repairing Imported Data

## Practice Objectives

- Set the import options to retrieve data from an .IGS file.
- Review the Translation Report that is generated when an .IGS file is imported.
- Transfer the imported .IGS data into the Repair environment and conduct a quality check for errors in the imported geometry.
- Appropriately set the stitch tolerance value so that gaps in the imported geometry can be automatically stitched.
- Use the Repair environment commands to repair gaps, delete and replace surfaces to successfully create a solid from the imported geometry.

In this practice, you import an IGES file, analyze it, and repair the surfaces. Once you finish repairing the surfaces to obtain a fully enclosed surface, you stitch it to obtain the solid model shown in Figure 3–9.

**Figure 3–9**

## Task 1 - Import the IGES file.

1. In the Quick Access Toolbar, click ![folder icon]. Select **import_surf.igs**. Click **Open**. The Import dialog box opens.

2. In the *Object Filters* area, select **Solids** and **Surfaces** and leave the other options in this area cleared, as shown in Figure 3–10.

3. Maintain the default in the *Inventor Length Units* area.

4. In the *Part Options* area, select **Composite**, as shown in Figure 3–10.

5. By default, the file is created in the working directory. You can use the browse button in the *Files Location* area to change directories, if required. You can also add a prefix or suffix to the filename, as shown in Figure 3–10. For this file, leave the *Name* field empty and the *File Location* as default.

**Figure 3–10**

6. Click **OK** to import the IGES file. The Model browser and model appear as shown in Figure 3–11.

import_surf.ipt
3rd Party
Surface Bodies(1)
View: Master
Origin
Composite 1
End of Part

**Figure 3–11**

## Task 2 - Examine the translation report.

Examine the translation report that is generated to review information such as the translation type, translation options used, component names, system from which the file was created, and success status.

1. In the Model browser, expand the **3rd Party** node and double-click on **import_surf.htm** to open and review the translation information.

2. Close the translation report window.

## Task 3 - Examine the Model Browser.

Examine the Model browser to determine what has been imported. This helps determine what is required with the model.

1. The import file contains a single composite surface. No solids have been imported (otherwise a feature named **Base1** would display in the Model browser).

## Task 4 - Perform a quality check to find errors in the imported geometry.

1. In the Model browser, right-click on **Composite1** and select **Repair Bodies**. The *Repair* tab displays.

2. In the Repair panel, click (Find Errors). The Find Errors dialog box opens. Click **Select All** to select all the Bodies in the imported geometry. Click **OK** to run the check. The bodies are analyzed and no problems are reported. If problems were reported they would be identified with symbols in the Model browser.

## Task 5 - Perform a preliminary stitch.

Perform a preliminary stitch to close up any insignificant gaps that might have resulted from the import and to help locate the significant gaps and over-extended surfaces. Use a small tolerance to avoid undesirable changes in the geometry.

1. In the Modify panel, click (Stitch). The Stitch dialog box opens.

2. Drag a bounding box around all of the geometry to select it. Ninety four (94) faces are selected.

3. Change the *Fill gaps smaller than* value to **0.05 mm**.

4. Click (Find remaining gaps and free edges). The Stitch dialog box and model display as shown in Figure 3–12.

   - Edges that could not be stitched (due to them being further apart than the defined maximum tolerance of 0.05 mm) are highlighted in the model and are listed in the Stitch dialog box.

   - Edges that were less than 0.05 mm apart have been stitched together.

   - There are 5 remaining free edges. To determine which edge in the model corresponds to which edge listed in the dialog box, select a row in the list. The corresponding edge highlights in blue on the model. Some of the edges are small and so you need to zoom in to see them.

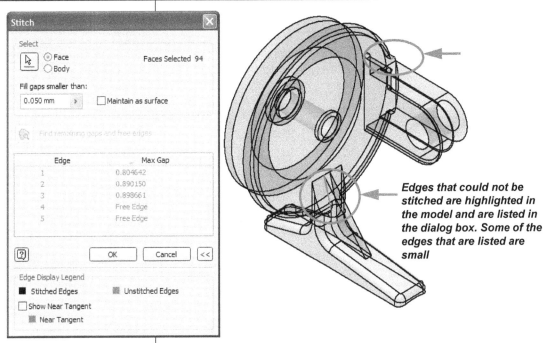

*Edges that could not be stitched are highlighted in the model and are listed in the dialog box. Some of the edges that are listed are small*

**Figure 3–12**

5. While keeping the Stitch dialog box open, rotate and zoom in on the model to get a better look at the highlighted edges that need to be resolved before the model can become solid. Some surface edges extend further than required and some adjacent surfaces contain a gap between them. There are two areas on the model (which contain the problem edges) that need to be repaired.

6. Click **OK** to close the Stitch dialog box. Note in the Model browser, the imported surface body has been changed to a single quilt because the surfaces were stitched together, as shown in Figure 3–13. However, the gaps between surfaces still remain.

**Figure 3–13**

### Task 6 - Use Extract Loop and then Boundary Trim.

In this task, you use **Extract Loop** to extend the edges and then **Boundary Trim** to trim back the surface to the required boundary.

1. Reorient the model and zoom as shown in Figure 3–14.

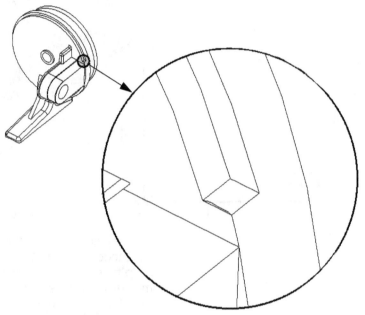

**Figure 3–14**

2. Position the cursor over the surface shown in Figure 3–15 in Shaded display mode to get a better idea of what needs to be repaired. Note that a gap exists.

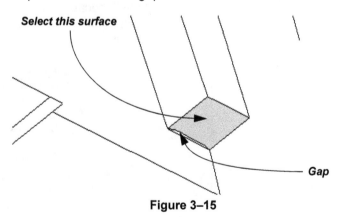

*Select this surface*

*Gap*

**Figure 3–15**

3. In the Modify panel, click ▣ (Extract Loop) to extend the surface.

4. Select the loop by selecting the surface shown in Figure 3–16.

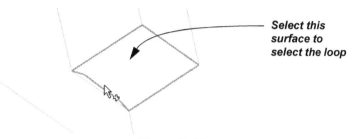

*Select this surface to select the loop*

**Figure 3–16**

5. Select **Delete Wires** to delete the original loop of the surface.

6. Click **Apply** and then click **Done**. The surface edges are extended, as shown in Figure 3–17.

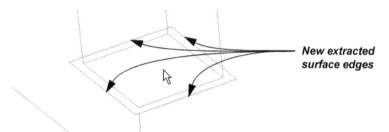

*New extracted surface edges*

**Figure 3–17**

7. In the Modify panel, click ▨ (Boundary Trim).

8. Select the edges shown in Figure 3–18 as the cutting edges.

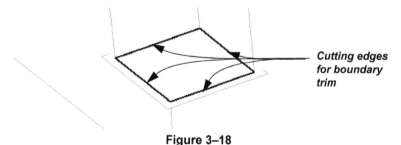

*Cutting edges for boundary trim*

**Figure 3–18**

*If an incorrect surface is selected, hold <Ctrl> and select the surface to clear it.*

9.  Click 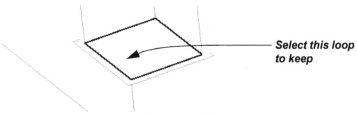 (Face or Loop) and select the loop to keep, as shown in Figure 3–19. Verify that the required loop is selected and is displayed in green, otherwise the incorrect portion of the surface is trimmed.

Select this loop to keep

**Figure 3–19**

10. Click **Apply** and then click **Done**. The surface is trimmed, as shown in Figure 3–20.

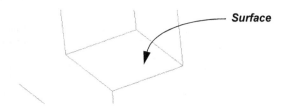

Surface

**Figure 3–20**

### Task 7 - Use Extract Loop and Boundary Trim a second time.

1.  Reorient the model and zoom, as shown in Figure 3–21.

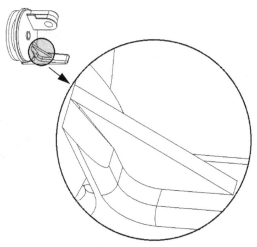

**Figure 3–21**

2. Position the cursor over the surfaces shown in Figure 3–22 to help visualize what needs to be repaired. Note the gap that exists between the surfaces.

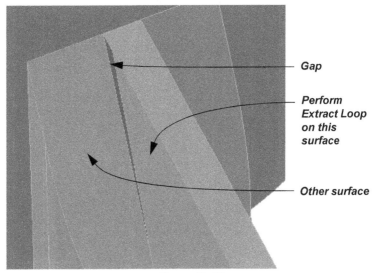

*Gap*

*Perform Extract Loop on this surface*

*Other surface*

**Figure 3–22**

3. With **Delete Wires** selected, use **Extract Loop** to obtain the surface shown in Figure 3–23.

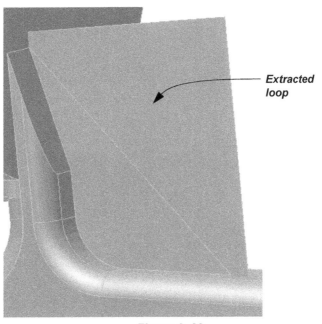

*Extracted loop*

**Figure 3–23**

4. Perform a Boundary Trim and select the edges shown in Figure 3–24 as the cutting edges.

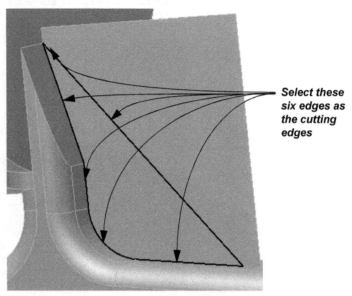

*Select these six edges as the cutting edges*

**Figure 3–24**

5. Select the Face or Loop reference, within the area to be kept, so that the model is trimmed as shown in Figure 3–25. Note that the gap no longer exists.

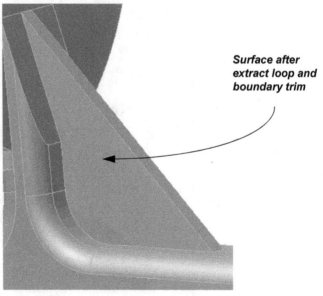

*Surface after extract loop and boundary trim*

**Figure 3–25**

## Task 8 - Stitch the surfaces.

1.  In the Modify panel, click 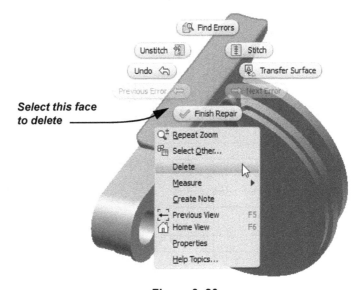(Stitch).

2.  In the *Select* area, select **Body**. Select the model. Now that the model is a Quilt, the **Face** option cannot be used to select the geometry.

3.  Verify that the *Fill gaps smaller than:* value is still set to **0.05 mm**.

4.  Click (Find remaining gaps and free edges). No open edges remain in the model and it is automatically converted into a solid.

5.  Click **OK**.

## Task 9 - Delete a surface from the stitched quilt.

The design intent of the model requires that the base be longer. In this task, you delete one of the faces that has been combined to create the current solid.

1.  Reorient the model so that you can see the bottom surface of the model. Right-click on the bottom face and select **Delete**, as shown in Figure 3–26.

**Figure 3–26**

## Task 10 - Stitch the surfaces.

In this task you will extend an existing surface and create a new surface to replace the one that was deleted.

1.  Reorient the model so that you can see the bottom surface of the model.

2.  In the Modify panel, click ⊞ (Extend Faces).

3.  Select the closed loop edge that represents the base of the model, as shown in Figure 3–27.

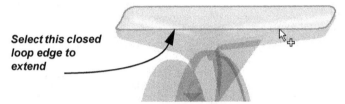

**Select this closed loop edge to extend**

**Figure 3–27**

4.  Set the extend distance to **2**. Click **Apply** and then click **Done**.

5.  In the Modify panel, click ⌐ (Boundary Patch).

6.  Select the extended edge as the reference for the Boundary Patch, as shown in Figure 3–28.

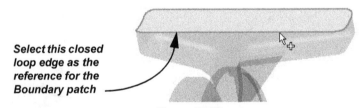

**Select this closed loop edge as the reference for the Boundary patch**

**Figure 3–28**

7.  Click **Apply** to create the new surface. Click **Done** to close the dialog box.

## Task 11 - Add the new surface to the stitched quilt.

In this task you will add the newly created surface to the model.

*As an alternative you can also right-click on the newly created bottom surface of the model and select **Add Surface**.*

1. In the Model browser, in the repair node, right-click on **Quilt3** and select **Add Surface**. The Stitch: Add dialog box opens.

2. In the *Select* area, select **Body** and select the existing quilted surface body.

3. Change the *Fill gaps smaller than:* value to **0.05 mm**.

4. Click (Find remaining gaps and free edges). No open edges should be reported.

5. Click **OK**.

6. In the Exit panel, click (Finish Repair) to exit the Repair environment. You are now placed in the standard part environment and can perform any regular operation on the solid model.

   The model becomes a solid with the addition of the cap surface, as shown in Figure 3–29. The **Surface Bodies** node has now been changed to a **Solid Bodies** node, identifying that the model is now a solid.

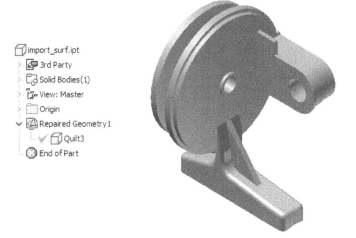

**Figure 3–29**

7. Save and close the model.

# Practice 3b

# Manipulating Imported Surfaces

### Practice Objectives

- Set the options to import data from a CATIA file.
- Appropriately set the stitch tolerance value so that gaps in the imported geometry can be automatically stitched to create a solid.
- Manipulate the resulting solid model using the surface Patch and Sculpt commands to add and remove solid geometry.

In this practice, you work with a file that has been imported from CATIA V5. You will import the geometry and then modify and remove features. The final part is shown in Figure 3–30.

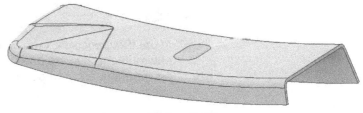

Figure 3–30

### Task 1 - Open a CATIA file.

1. In the Quick Access Toolbar, click . Ensure that the Files of type drop-down list is set to display all files or CATIA V5 files. Select **Trim_Panel.CATPart**. Click **Open**. The Import dialog box opens.

2. In the *Import Type* area, select **Convert Model** to convert the model without keeping any associative links to the CATIA file.

3. In the *Object Filters* area, select **Solids** and **Surfaces**. Leave the other options in this area cleared.

4. Maintain the default in the *Inventor Length Units* area.

5. In the *Part Options* area, select **Composite**.

6. Maintain the defaults in the *File Names* area.

7. In the *Select* tab, click **Load Model**. The model preview displays, as shown in Figure 3–31. Individual surfaces cannot be added or removed for this model. Surface manipulation for this CATIA part can be done in the Repair Environment.

**Figure 3–31**

8. Click **OK** to close the dialog box and import the geometry.

---

**Task 2 - Stitch the Trim_Panel.CATPart file.**

---

In this task, you switch to the Repair environment and stitch together the imported surfaces.

1. In the Model browser, right-click on **Composite1** and select **Repair Bodies**. The *Repair* tab displays.

2. In the Modify panel, click (Stitch). The Stitch dialog box opens.

3. Drag a bounding box around all of the geometry to select all 29 faces.

4. In the *Fill gaps smaller than:* field, leave the default value.

5. Click (Find remaining gaps and free edges). No open edges are reported. Only free edges are located around the exterior of the model.

6. Click **OK** to close the Stitch dialog box.

7. In the Exit panel, click (Finish Repair) to exit the Repair environment. You are now placed in the standard part environment and can perform any regular operation on the model.

## Task 3 - Use the Thicken/Offset command to create a solid.

1. In the Modify panel, click 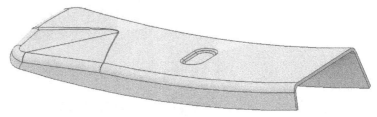 (Thicken/Offset). The Thicken/Offset dialog box displays.

2. Select **Quilt** to easily select the stitched surface.

3. Select the stitched surface and enter a distance of **4 mm**.

4. Click **OK**. The model displays as shown in Figure 3–32.

*Figure 3–32*

## Task 4 - Modify surfaces to incorporate design intent.

In this task you will create four boundary patch surfaces that will be used to modify the model.

1. Right-click on the **Repaired Geometry1** node in the Model browser and select **Repair Bodies**. Alternatively, double-click on the node.

2. Select the nine surfaces that make up the indented area shown in Figure 3–33. Right-click and select **Delete** to remove them from the surface.

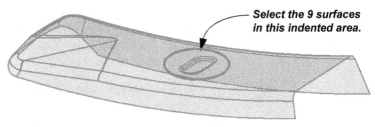

Select the 9 surfaces in this indented area.

*Figure 3–33*

3. In the Modify panel, click  (Boundary Patch).

4. Select the loop of edges that remain once the surfaces have been deleted as the reference for the Boundary Patch.

5. Click **Apply** to create the new surface. Click **Done** to close the dialog box.

6. In the Model browser, in the repair node, right-click on **Quilt2** and select **Add Surface**. The Stitch: Add dialog box opens.

7. In the *Select* area, select **Body** and select the existing quilted surface body.

8. Change the *Fill gaps smaller than:* value to **0.05 mm**.

9. Click 🔍 (Find remaining gaps and free edges). Eleven open edges should be reported. These are the outside edges of the surface.

10. Click **OK**.

11. In the Exit panel, click ✓ (Finish Repair) to exit the Repair environment.

12. The Thicken feature might fail due to the changes in the surface. If so, click **Accept**.

*Consider using the **Adjust** tool to manipulate the color of the new boundary patch so that it matches the rest of the model.*

13. Double-click on the **Thicken1** feature in the Model browser to edit it and select the reference surface again. The reference was lost when the modification was made. Click **OK**. The model displays as shown in Figure 3–34.

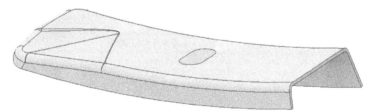

**Figure 3–34**

14. Save the model.

# Chapter Review Questions

1.  How can you bring imported data into the Repair environment, if it is not already imported into this environment?

    a.  Right-click on the imported data and select **Repair Bodies**.

    b.  Right-click on the imported data and select **Copy to Repair**.

    c.  This cannot be done. It must be done during import.

2.  In the Repair environment, which option can you use to close small gaps between surfaces?

    a.  Extend Faces

    b.  Intersect Faces

    c.  Stitch

    d.  Unstitch

    e.  Boundary Trim

3.  Which two commands function in the same way except that when one of the commands is executed, you specify a destination body?

    a.  Stitch

    b.  Transfer Surface

    c.  Unstitch

    d.  Boundary Patch

    e.  Boundary Trim

    f.  Extend Faces

4.  In the Repair environment, which option can you use to create a new surface referencing a closed set of adjacent edges?

    a.  Extend Faces

    b.  Intersect Faces

    c.  Boundary Trim

    d.  Boundary Patch

    e.  Extract Loop

5. Match the error types in the left column to its symbol that identifies their type in the right column.

| Error Types | Icon | Answer |
|---|---|---|
| a. Geometry that contains errors | ✔ | _____ |
| b. Geometry needing further investigation | ⓘ | _____ |
| c. Healthy geometry | ⚠ | _____ |

# Command Summary

| Button | Command | Location |
|---|---|---|
| N/A | Add Surface | • **Context menu:** In graphics window<br>• **Context menu:** In Model browser with surface selected |
| | Boundary Patch | • **Ribbon:** *Repair* tab>Modify panel |
| | Boundary Trim | • **Ribbon:** *Repair* tab>Modify panel |
| | Edit Regions | • **Ribbon:** *Repair* tab>Modify panel |
| | Extend Faces | • **Ribbon:** *Repair* tab>Modify panel |
| | Extract Loop | • **Ribbon:** *Repair* tab>Modify panel |
| | Find Errors | • **Ribbon:** *Repair* tab>Repair panel<br>• **Context menu:** In graphics window |
| | Finish Repair | • **Ribbon:** *Repair* tab>Exit panel<br>• **Context menu:** In graphics window |
| | Heal Errors | • **Ribbon:** *Repair* tab>Repair panel |
| | Intersect Faces | • **Ribbon:** *Repair* tab>Modify panel |
| | Next Error | • **Ribbon:** *Repair* tab>Repair panel<br>• **Context menu:** In graphics window |
| | Previous Error | • **Ribbon:** *Repair* tab>Repair panel<br>• **Context menu:** In graphics window |
| | Repair Bodies | • **Ribbon:** *3D Model* tab>Surface panel<br>• **Context menu:** In Model browser with repair node selected |
| | Reverse Normal | • **Ribbon:** *Repair* tab>Modify panel |
| | Stitch | • **Ribbon:** *Repair* tab>Modify panel<br>• **Context menu:** In graphics window |
| | Transfer Surface | • **Ribbon:** *Repair* tab>Modify panel<br>• **Context menu:** In graphics window |
| | Unstitch | • **Ribbon:** *Repair* tab>Modify panel<br>• **Context menu:** In graphics window |

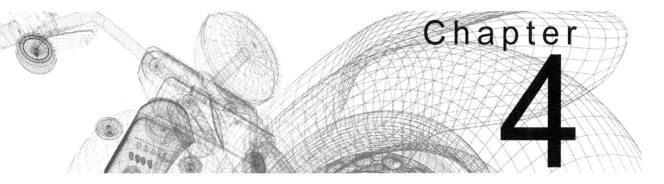

# Importing AutoCAD Data

There are several ways to incorporate AutoCAD® DWG files in an Autodesk® Inventor® file. The method you use depends on your project requirements. You can open the file directly in the Autodesk Inventor software for review. You can also import and convert the AutoCAD DWG into an Inventor DWG file, where all links to the original AutoCAD DWG file are lost.

## Learning Objectives in this Chapter

- Open an AutoCAD DWG file directly into an Autodesk Inventor part file and review the data.
- Use the DWG/DXF File Wizard and its options to import files into an Autodesk Inventor file.

# 4.1 Opening AutoCAD Files

When an AutoCAD DWG file is selected for opening, you can either open the file directly or import it so that it is converted to an Autodesk Inventor DWG file. These two options represent two of the methods that can be used to view and use AutoCAD DWG files in the Autodesk Inventor software.

## Opening DWG Files

By default, when a DWG file is opened using the Open dialog box, the file is opened directly in Autodesk Inventor. The file remains in a native AutoCAD DWG format, enabling you to view, plot, and measure the file contents. Objects display exactly as they do in AutoCAD. If changes to the DWG file are required, you should make the changes directly in the AutoCAD software. Figure 4–1 shows an example of the YA-Base.dwg AutoCAD file that has been opened in Autodesk Inventor. You can double-click on each of the nodes in the Model browser to activate the opened model, sheet, or layouts.

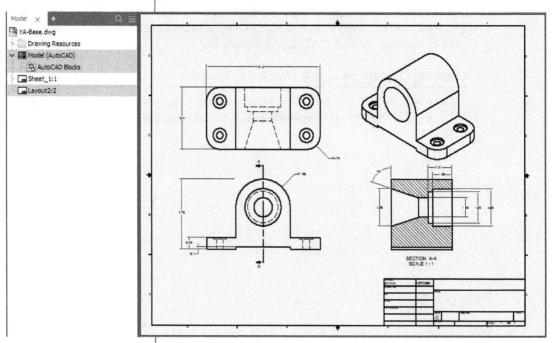

Figure 4–1

# Importing DWG Files

To convert the AutoCAD DWG to a native Autodesk Inventor DWG file, the DWG/DXF File Wizard is used. The data is imported and any associative link between the source and new file are lost. When importing, you have the ability to customize many options as well as the layers that are imported.

## How To: Import an Autodesk DWG File Using the DWG/DXF File Wizard

1. In the **File** menu, in the *Get Started* tab or the Quick Access Toolbar, select **Open**. The Open dialog box opens.
2. Select **DWG Files** from the Files of type drop-down list. DXF files can also be imported using the wizard
3. Select the Autodesk file to import, and click **Options**.
4. In the File Open Options dialog box (shown in Figure 4–2), select **Import** and click **OK**.

*Consider using the **Import DWG** option in the expanded **Open** command on the **File** menu to avoid using the File Open Options dialog box.*

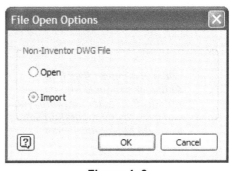

**Figure 4–2**

5. Click **Open**. The DWG/DXF File Wizard dialog box opens similar to that shown in Figure 4–3.

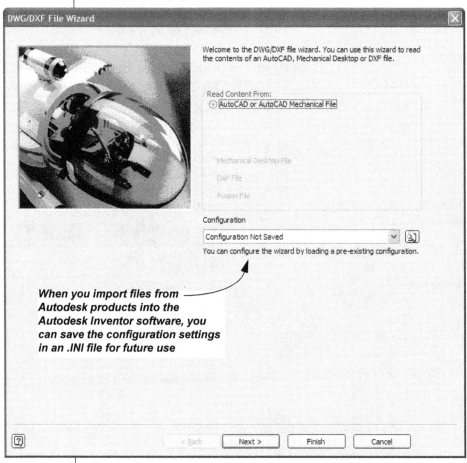

When you import files from Autodesk products into the Autodesk Inventor software, you can save the configuration settings in an .INI file for future use

**Figure 4–3**

*The settings you define in this wizard can be saved as a configuration file and used by during future imports.*

6. In the *Read Content From* area, verify that the correct file format is selected for import. Specify a configuration file to use, as required. To use the settings defined in the selected configuration file or to accept the default file settings, click **Finish**. To continue defining import options, click **Next**.

The Layers and Objects Import Options dialog box opens. The dialog box varies depending on the file format being imported. Figure 4–4 shows the options for the import of a DXF, AutoCAD DWG, or AutoCAD Mechanical DWG file.

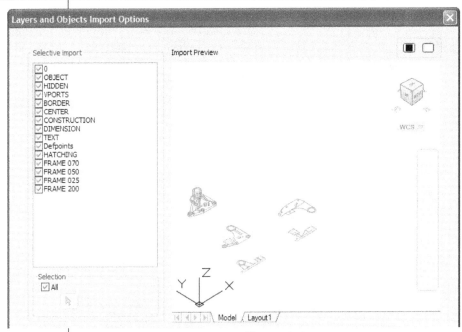

**Figure 4–4**

7. The Layers and Objects Import Options dialog box enables you to specify what data to translate.

   For an AutoCAD DWG file:

   - Use the *Import Preview* area to view the data. Right-click or use the Navigation toolbar to access view manipulation options or the right-click to access file options.
   - Select the data to import by selecting layers to include from the Selective import area or select specific entities to include by deactivating the **All** option in the *Selection* area and selecting entities in the Import preview area.

   For a Mechanical Desktop DWG file:

   - Use **Parts and Assemblies** to import parts and assemblies into the Autodesk Inventor software, as required.
   - Use **All Layouts as Drawings with Views** to import AutoCAD layouts into drawing views and annotations.
   - Use the **Selected Layout as Drawings with Draft Views** options to import the selected layout into an Autodesk Inventor drawing. This option is only available when a layout tab is selected and the **All Layouts as Drawings with Views** option is cleared.

8. Click **Next** when finished defining the options. The Import Destination Options dialog box opens.

9. The Import Destination Options dialog box for Mechanical Desktop DWG files also differs from the dialog box for DXF and other DWG files. Figure 4–5 shows the options that are available during the import of a DXF, AutoCAD DWG, or AutoCAD Mechanical DWG file.

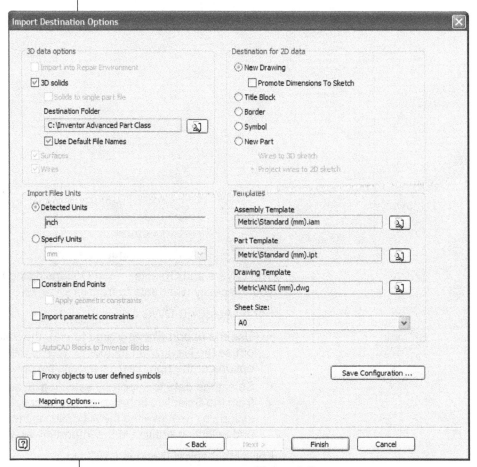

**Figure 4–5**

For DXF and other non-Mechanical Desktop DWG files, the available options are:

- Activate the **3D solids** option to import the 3D solids from AutoCAD, otherwise, they are not included. If **Surfaces** or **Wires** exist in the imported file you can select these options, if required on import. Selecting a destination folder specifies the directory in which new Autodesk Inventor files are created as a result of importing 3D solids. Select the **Use Default File Names** option to automatically name new files based on the name of the DWG file.

*Select the **Map all layers and dimensions to a single sketch** option in the Mapping Options dialog box to avoid creating as many sketches as you have layers.*

- Specify the units to use in the *Import Files Units* area.
- Select **Constrain End Points** to automatically apply endpoint constraints. Clear this option to manually assign them. Use **Apply geometric constraints** to fully constrain the sketch.
- Select the **Import parametric constraints** option to translate 2D parametric constraints into a sketch.
- Select **AutoCAD Blocks to Inventor Blocks** to import AutoCAD blocks as sketch blocks when opened in an Autodesk Inventor sketch.
- Select **Proxy objects to user defined symbols** to import proxy objects from AutoCAD for use as custom symbols.
- Click **Mapping Options** to set the mapping of layers and fonts.
- Select **New Drawing** to import the 2D data on the layouts into a new drawing file. Imported 2D geometry is placed in sketches attached to a draft view. Dimensions are placed in the sketch containing the associated geometry. Unassociated dimensions, symbols, and other annotations are imported onto the drawing sheet. Blocks are imported as sketched symbols and placed in the *Drawing Resources* folder.
- Select **Promote Dimensions To Sketch** to import dimensions as sketch dimensions on a sheet in a drawing file. The promoted dimensions are associative and change if the sketch geometry is modified.
- Select **Title Block** to import 2D data from the selected layers into the title block in a new drawing file.
- Select **Border** to import 2D data from the selected layers into the border in a new drawing file.
- Select **Symbol** to import 2D data from the selected layers into a sketched symbol under the *Drawing Resources* folder in a new drawing file. An instance of the sketched symbol is also placed on the first sheet in the drawing.
- Select **New Part** to import 2D geometry from model space or paper space into a sketch in a new part. Associated dimensions are imported into the sketch, but unassociated dimensions, symbols, and other annotations are not imported.
- Select the drawing, part and assembly template files to use when new files are created during import. Also, specify the sheet size to use for new drawings.
- Click **Save Configuration** to reuse the same import settings in the future.

For Mechanical Desktop DWG files, many of the Import Destination options are the same as those available when importing DXF and other non-Mechanical Desktop DWG files. The options that are different include the following:

- Specifying **Referenced components only** or **All component definitions** for assemblies. You can also control whether to discard the .IAM file for any single part assemblies.
- Specifying whether to **Translate body only** or **As features**. For Mechanical Desktop files with unsupported features you can select the additional options.
- Importing only the selected file or external files as well for drawings with view options.
- Specifying the options for mapping mechanical symbols.
- Overwriting duplicate files that are found or using the existing file that is found.

10. Click **Finish** when you are done setting the import options and to begin the import.

Depending on the information in the AutoCAD file, the import produces different results in the form or model layouts, sheets, and imported base geometry. Consider the following:

- If you want to use 2D AutoCAD data to create features in a part, you can import the DWG file into a new part file (.IPT) or into a sketch in an active part. Alternatively, you can open the DWG and copy views to help create solid geometry. Dwg Underlays can also be used and are discussed in the next section.

- Materials applied in an AutoCAD DWG are maintained in the Autodesk Inventor software after translation. To view the materials, set the Visual Style for the part to **Realistic**.

- For AutoCAD 3D solids, they are imported as Autodesk solid bodies into an Autodesk Inventor part file (.IPT). When multiple solids are translated, a part file is created for each body and an assembly file that contains references to each part is created. AutoCAD 3D solids are not parametric, so they are brought in as non-parametric solid bodies without separately defined features (i.e., boundary representations).

# 4.2 Working with other Autodesk Product Files

Other Autodesk software products can also be used in Autodesk Inventor. This section discusses some of the options you have when using other Autodesk product files in the Autodesk Inventor software.

## Mechanical Desktop

You can open or import Autodesk Mechanical Desktop DWG files, just like AutoCAD DWG files, as follows:

- Opening a DWG provides a Model and Layout. Using a Model view you can zoom, pan, rotate, measure, and print. While using the Layout you can add views or annotations.

- Importing a DWG using the File Wizard creates a parametric part with parametric features. Some data might not be converted and would need to be recreated

- Parts can be placed in Autodesk Inventor assemblies using Place Component. A link is maintained so that any updates are reflected.

*To translate files to the Autodesk Inventor software, the Autodesk Mechanical Desktop software must be installed.*

## Alias Studio Files

The Autodesk® Alias® files can be opened directly in the Autodesk Inventor software using the File Open dialog box either by importing, or by dragging and dropping the .WIRE file from Windows Explorer into a file. Once opened, you can use modeling tools to manipulate the geometry. Imported data maintains links with the original Alias data.

## Autodesk Revit Files

The Autodesk® Revit® interoperability functionality enables you to import an Autodesk Revit file (.RVT) or place a file as a component in a Autodesk Inventor assembly file using the Place Component dialog box. When inserting, you are prompted to import the data as a single composite feature or as a multi-body. Changes that are made in the source model can be updated in the Autodesk Inventor file.

## 3ds Max Design Files

3ds Max files must be exported as a .SAT file before you are able to import it into Autodesk Inventor. There is no associativity between the imported data and the 3ds Max file. If changes are made in 3ds Max, the file must be re-imported into Autodesk Inventor.

# Practice 4a

# Import an AutoCAD DWG File into Autodesk Inventor

### Practice Objective

- Use the DWG/DXF File Wizard to import an AutoCAD DWG file into an Autodesk Inventor part file and work with the data.

In this practice, you will import an AutoCAD DWG file directly into Autodesk Inventor. The AutoCAD DWG file contains a 3D AutoCAD model and a 2D layout. Once imported, you will review the file and use copy and paste techniques to copy non-associative 2D drawing data into a new Inventor model. The AutoCAD 3D model and drawing are shown in Figure 4–6.

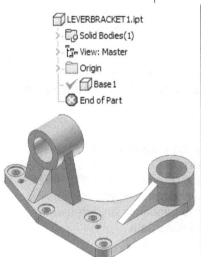

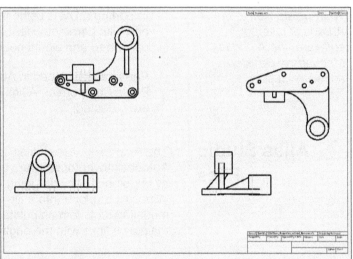

**Figure 4–6**

---

### Task 1 - Import the AutoCAD DWG file.

1. In the Quick Access Toolbar, click .

2. In the File of type drop-down list, select **AutoCAD Dwg Files**.

3. Select **LEVERBRACKET.dwg** and click **Options**. The File Open Options dialog box opens. It enables you to directly open the DWG file in the Autodesk Inventor software or you can import the file. In this practice you will import the drawing.

4. Select **Import** and click **OK**.

---

5. Click **Open**. The DWG/DXF File Wizard displays.

6. In the *Read Content From* area, keep the **AutoCAD or AutoCAD Mechanical File** option selected. Leave the **Configuration** option set to **Configuration Not Saved** as you have not yet saved a configuration file. Click **Next**. The Layers and Objects Import Options dialog box opens. A preview of the AutoCAD 3D Solid geometry and its views are shown.

*You can also zoom in and out using the scroll wheel.*

7. In the dialog box, in the top right corner, click ☐ to change the background to white. You can use the Navigation bar or right-click on the background of the preview window to access the view orientation and manipulation options (e.g., pan, zoom). Manipulate the model as required.

The Layers and Objects Import Options dialog box is shown in Figure 4–7.

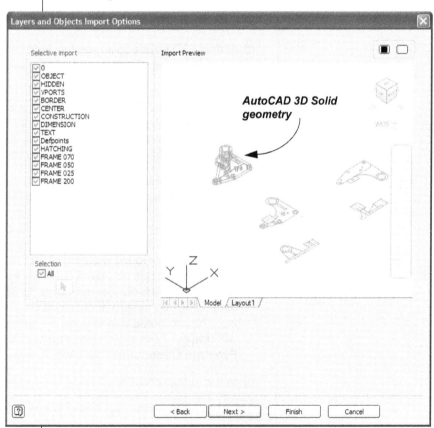

**Figure 4–7**

8. In the Navigation Bar, click to fit the entire drawing in the preview area.

9. Clear **OBJECT**. Note that the model entities are removed.

10. Clear **HIDDEN** to remove the hidden lines.

11. Select **OBJECT** and **HIDDEN** again so that those entities will be imported.

12. To import specific entities from the DWG, in the *Selection* area, you can clear the **All** option and select individual entities to import. Leave the **All** option selected.

13. Select the *Layout1* tab to review the layout that will be imported.

14. Return to the *Model* tab.

15. Click **Next**. The Import Destination Options dialog box opens.

16. Activate **3D solids** to import the AutoCAD 3D solids that exist in the DWG file. Clear the **Solids to single part file** option, if selected.

17. In the *3D data options* area, verify that the *Destination Folder* field is set to the practice files directory. This is the directory where the new files will be created as a result of the import. Also verify that **Use Default File Names** is activated.

18. Select **New Drawing** to import the 2D data on the layouts into a new Autodesk Inventor drawing file. Imported 2D geometry is placed in sketches attached to a draft view. Dimensions are placed in the sketch containing the associated geometry. Unassociated dimensions, symbols, and other annotations are imported onto the drawing sheet. Blocks are imported as sketched symbols and placed in the *Drawing Resources* folder. The **Promote Dimensions To Sketch** option imports dimensions as sketch dimensions on a sheet in a drawing file. The promoted dimensions are associative and so they will change if the sketch geometry is modified. Deactivate **Promote Dimensions To Sketch**, if enabled.

19. In the *Templates* area, next to the Assembly Template, click . In the *Metric* tab, select **Standard(mm).iam**.

20. For the Part Template, in the *Metric* tab, select **Standard(mm).ipt**.

21. For the Drawing Template, in the *Metric* tab, select **ANSI(mm).dwg**.

22. For the *Sheet Size*, select **A0**.

23. Click **Save Configuration** and enter **AutoCAD 3D Solid using metric** as the filename. Save it in the practice files directory.

24. Click **Finish** to begin the import. The DWG data is imported as a new part and drawing file.

25. Activate the LEVERBRACKET1 part file window by selecting it from the tabs along the bottom of the graphics window.

26. Return to the model's Home view using the ViewCube.

27. The color is imported from the source AutoCAD file. Change the default appearance to **Steel** using the Appearance Override drop-down list in the Quick Access toolbar, to display the model in a better color.

28. The model displays as shown in Figure 4–8. The model is a solid feature, but it is a boundary representation (rather than being made up of several features). You can now edit the solid using **Edit Solid** or **Direct Edit,** or add and remove material from the solid and use any of the edges and faces as references as you would a regular native Autodesk Inventor solid.

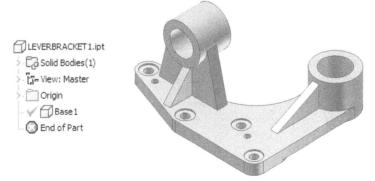

**Figure 4–8**

29. Save the part file using the default name.

## Task 2 - Review and edit the imported drawing.

1. In the **Drawing1.dwg** drawing, expand the *Drawing Resources* folder and **Sketch Symbols** node. Right-click on ISO A2 title block and select **Insert**. Place the title block on the drawing. Click **OK** to leave the title block entries blank. Right-click and select **Cancel** to cancel placing additional title blocks.

2. The title block is small compared to sheet. To change the size, right-click on the title block, select **Edit Symbol**, enter **2** for the *Scale*, and click **OK**.

3. Use the green dot at the center of the title block to drag it to fit. Select any geometry on a view and drag it to reposition all of the views on the drawing sheet. You might have to also reposition the title block. The drawing displays as shown in Figure 4–9.

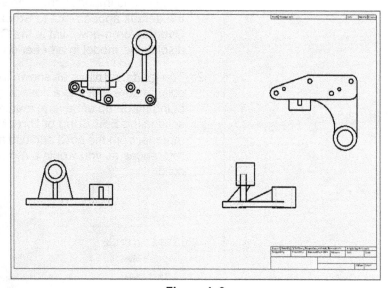

**Figure 4–9**

4. In the Model browser, expand the **Sheet:1** and the **ImportDraftView** branches. The 2D entities were imported into sketches, so the drawing views are actually sketched entities rather than views, unlike those in regular native Autodesk Inventor drawings.

5. Save the drawing as **Leverbracket2.dwg** and save it in the practice files directory. Close the files.

# Practice 4b

# Open AutoCAD DWG Data to Create a Solid

### Practice Objective

- Open an AutoCAD DWG file directly into an Autodesk Inventor part file and work with the data.

In this practice, you will open an AutoCAD DWG file in Autodesk Inventor. You will review the contents of the DWG file and use some of its 2D data to create a sketch in new Autodesk Inventor file that can be used to create the initial geometry for an Inventor model. The geometry that will be created is shown in Figure 4–10.

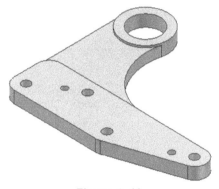

**Figure 4–10**

### Task 1 - Open an AutoCAD DWG and view the data in Autodesk Inventor.

1. In the Quick Access Toolbar, click .

2. Select **LEVERBRACKET.dwg** and click **Options**. The File Open Options dialog box opens.

3. By default, **Open** is already selected. If not, select **Open** and click **OK**.

4. Click **Open**. The **Leverbracket.dwg** file and the Browser display as shown in Figure 4–11.

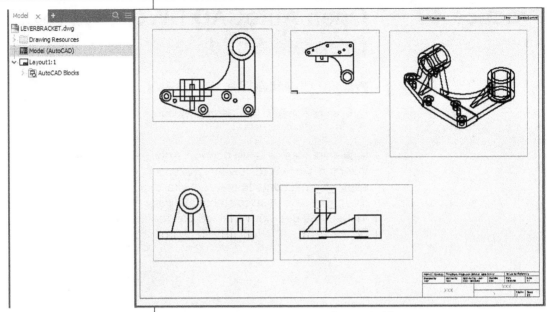

**Figure 4–11**

5.  In the Model browser, double-click on the **Model (AutoCAD)** node. Click **Yes** and accept the error report. You will just be copying data from the file.

6.  To change the display color of the background, in the Model browser, right-click on **Model** and select **Background Color**. Change the color to white. The model displays as shown in Figure 4–12.

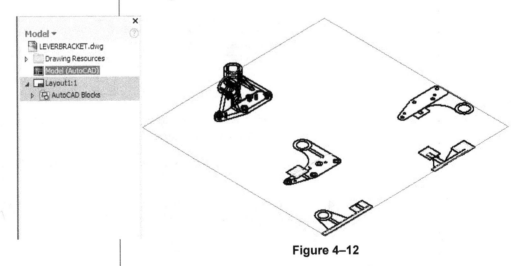

**Figure 4–12**

### Task 2 - Use the AutoCAD DWG data to create an Autodesk Inventor part file.

1. Select and drag a selection box around the top right view, as shown in Figure 4–13.

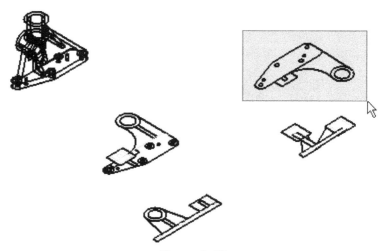

Figure 4–13

2. Right-click and select **Copy**.

3. Start a new part file using the **Standard (mm).ipt** metric template.

4. Create a sketch on the XY plane. Once you are placed in the Sketch environment, right-click and select **Paste**. Place the entities in the sketch.

5. In the Navigation Bar, click (Zoom All) to refit the model.

6. Use the **Rotate** and **Move** tools to move the entities relative to the origin center, as shown in Figure 4–14.

   **Hint**: You need to create construction lines and a point at the intersection of the construction lines. Once all the reference items are created you can move the entities to the projected origin center.

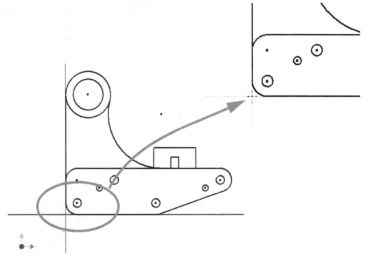

**Figure 4–14**

7. Project YZ and XZ and locate the geometry's horizontal bottom and vertical left side entities to lie on these projected planes.

8. For simplicity, dimension the remaining entities using **Auto Dimension**. Normally, it is recommended to place dimensions based on your required design intent, but for this practice you use this tool to quickly progress to creating geometry. Finish the sketch.

9. Create an Extrude and select the three closed sections of the sketch and the six holes to obtain the solid in Figure 4–15. Extrude the feature **16mm** and flip the creation direction below the sketch plane.

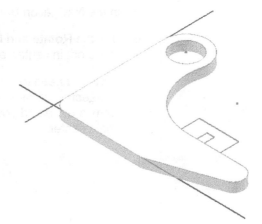

**Figure 4–15**

10. Expand **Extrusion1**. Right-click on **Sketch1** and select **Share Sketch**. Alternatively, you can select and drag **Sketch1** above the Extrusion to share it. By sharing the sketch it copies the sketch outside the extrusion for use with other features.

11. Toggle on the **Visibility** for the shared sketch, if it is off.

12. Extrude the two additional closed sections by **3mm**, as shown in Figure 4–16.

    **Hint:** When extruding the larger section you also need to select the six holes to create the solid. This enables you to then use the circular sections to create separate features later in the design process.

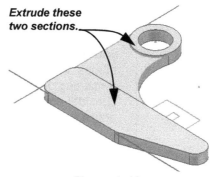

*Extrude these two sections.*

**Figure 4–16**

13. Create extruded cuts to represent the holes, as shown in Figure 4–17. The holes cut through the entire model. As an alternative, you could also have edited the sketch and added points to the centers of the holes. The points could then have been used with the **Hole** command to create the holes with the required diameters.

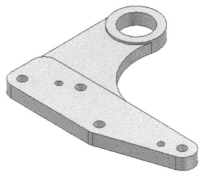

**Figure 4–17**

14. Save the part.

Up to this point, the method used to create the model is only one interpretation of how the model can be created. There are many other alternatives. For example, you can use the copied entities and create individual sketches for each feature, dimension and constrain them as required, and remove links to the original copied entities. Whichever method you use, consider your design intent and what information you need to communicate how the model is manufactured. Ultimately, because the data was copied from the AutoCAD file, it does not maintain any associative link.

**Optional Task - Continue modeling the solid geometry.**

After you have finished creating all of the practices in this chapter, continue to model the geometry for the leverbracket part that was originally created in the AutoCAD software. You can take measurements, as required, using the imported model that you created in Task 1. You need to create additional sketch planes and copy entities from the .DWG file to create the remaining geometry. In some situations you might want to consider creating features on your own instead of using copied entities.

# Chapter Review Questions

1. When using an AutoCAD .DWG file in Autodesk Inventor, which of the following Open Options should be used to view, plot, and measure the file contents?

   a. Open

   b. Import

2. Which of the following Open Options should be used to create a single solid-body base feature when an AutoCAD 3D DWG file is required for use in Autodesk Inventor?

   a. Open

   b. Import

3. Which of the following three methods for incorporating AutoCAD DWG data in Autodesk Inventor enables you to review sheets in the DWG file?

   a. Selecting **Open** in the File Open Options dialog box.

   b. Selecting **Import** in the File Open Options dialog box.

   c. Creating a new part file and selecting **Import** in the *3D Model* tab>Create panel.

4. Importing Alias wire files into Autodesk Inventor maintains as associative link with the source file.

   a. True

   b. False

# Command Summary

| Button | Command | Location |
|--------|---------|----------|
| Options... | **Options (import options)** | • **Ribbon:** *Get Started* tab>Launch panel>Open<br>• **File Menu:** Open dialog box<br>• **Quick Access toolbar:** Open dialog box |

# Working with DWG Underlays

As was discussed in the previous chapter, AutoCAD® DWG files can be both imported and opened directly into Autodesk® Inventor® file. Alternatively, you can also use an AutoCAD DWG as an associative underlay in an Autodesk Inventor file. Understanding the process and results of each of these methods helps you identify which is the best for your situation.

### Learning Objective in this Chapter

- Use an AutoCAD DWG file in an Autodesk Inventor part file so that the geometry created in Inventor remains associative with the AutoCAD DWG file.

# 5.1 DWG File Underlays

Importing an AutoCAD DWG file into an Autodesk Inventor part file enables you to import an associative underlay by referencing the AutoCAD DWG. The DWG underlay can be imported on one or more work planes or faces, enabling you to project it into sketches and use it to create associative geometry. If changes are made in the source AutoCAD DWG file, the change can be updated in the Autodesk Inventor file. Additionally, in assembly files, you can use constraints and joints to create relationships between a DWG underlay geometry and a part.

**Importing a DWG File as an Underlay**

### How To: Import an Autodesk DWG File as an Associative Underlay

1. Start a new part file using a template and save the file. A DWG file cannot be imported into a new, unsaved file.
2. In the *3D Model* tab>Create panel, click ⬆ (Import). Select and open an AutoCAD DWG file.
3. Select an origin plane or planar face to import the DWG file onto.
4. Select a origin point reference to locate the DWG file.
5. Click **OK** when prompted that inserting an AutoCAD DWG produces an associative underlay. The DWG file is listed in the Model browser as an independent node.

- To redefine the placement plane and origin point that was used to locate the file, right-click on the filename in the Model browser, and select **Redefine**, as shown in Figure 5–1. You are then prompted to select a new plane and origin point to locate the underlay file.

**Figure 5–1**

**Enhanced**
in **2018**

- To open the DWG file in AutoCAD, right-click on the underlay file name in the Model Browser and select **Open** in AutoCAD.

## Controlling Layer Visibility

Once a DWG file has been imported as an underlay, you can control its layer visibility.

### How To: Control the Layer Visibility

1. Right-click on the DWG file in the Model browser and select **Layer Visibility**. The Layer Visibility dialog box opens, as shown in Figure 5–2.

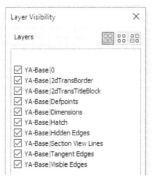

**Figure 5–2**

2. Toggle on/off the layer names to customize the data that will be imported.

   • Use the filter settings at the top of the dialog box to quickly clear, select all, or invert the selected layers.

   • The visibility of any of the layers can be controlled at any time using this dialog box.

3. Click **OK** to close the Layer Visibility dialog box.

## Moving an Underlay

If the imported file does not appear in the correct location relative to the model's origin, it can be translated.

### How To: Move a DWG Underlay

1. Right-click on the DWG file in the Model browser and select **Translate**. A translation triad is displayed on the selected origin point.

2. Using the mini-toolbar, move the AutoCAD DWG file relative to the model's origin, as required:

   • In the mini-toolbar, click **Locate** and select a new reference on the imported DWG file to reposition the triad.

   • In the mini-toolbar, click **Snap To** and select the Origin Center Point or another point to align the DWG underlay as required in the model.

3. Click ✓ to complete the translation.

## Cropping an Underlay

An imported DWG underlay can be cropped to simplify the amount of detail that is displayed. Cropping can also help improve performance.

### How To: Crop Entities in a DWG Underlay

1. Right-click on the DWG file in the Model browser and select **Crop**.
2. In the graphics window, drag a bounding box around the entities that you want to keep.
3. Right-click in the graphics window and select **OK (Enter)** to complete the crop. Any geometry that was not included in the selected area is automatically removed.

- Once an DWG underlay file is cropped, a **Crop** node is added to the Model Browser.

- Only one crop can be made to a file, thus if a change is required, you must delete the crop element. To delete a Crop, right-click on the element in the Model browser and select **Delete**.

## Using an Underlay to Create Geometry

To use the imported underlay to create solid geometry that remains associative to the AutoCAD DWG file, consider the following along with your standard sketching and feature creation techniques:

- Start the creation of a new sketch. In the *Sketch* tab>Create panel, expand the Project Geometry options and select

   (Project DWG Geometry). By projecting the DWG geometry you can maintain the reference between the sketch and the DWG file. Use the filter options in the mini-toolbar to project single geometry ( ), connected geometry ( ), or a DWG Block ( ). Click ⊗ to close the mini-toolbar and cancel the Project DWG Geometry command.

**Enhanced**
in 2018

- If the **Autoproject edges during curve creation** option is enabled in the Application Options>*Sketch* tab, some entities are automatically projected into a sketch. These entity types include points (start, mid, end, center points), arcs, circles, lines, and polylines. Cropped entities are not included.

- When projected, all of the entities are fully constrained. Consider creating Driven Dimensions to identify key dimensions in the underlay that can be used to drive solid geometry. For the example shown in Figure 5–3, the Driven Dimension can now be used to define the depth of the model.

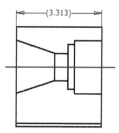

**Figure 5–3**

- In the Model Browser, right-click on the imported DWG file to access the **Suppress Link** and **Break Link** options. These options can be used to either temporarily break the link with the source DWG file (**Suppress Link**) or permanently break the link (**Break Link**).

An imported AutoCAD DWG file can also be used as a layout reference to assemble components in an Inventor assembly file. For the example shown in Figure 5–4, the factory floor layout is an AutoCAD DWG file that can be used for assembly references in a top-level assembly.

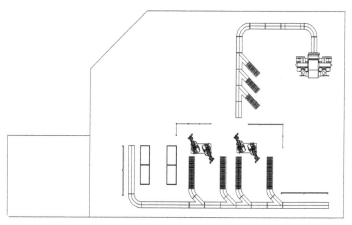

**Figure 5–4**

**Enhanced**
in **2018**

*As of the March 2017 software release, the **Translate** command is not available to modify the location of an underlay placed in an assembly. To rotate it on the placement plane, you can expand the **Relationships** node in the Model Browser and modify the **Angle 2** constraint, as required. As a workaround, insert the underlay into a part file, position it, and then insert the part into the assembly.*

• The underlay is placed in an assembly file as a placed component. Many of the right-click menu options that are available in the part environment to edit the underlay are also available in an assembly, as shown in Figure 5–5.

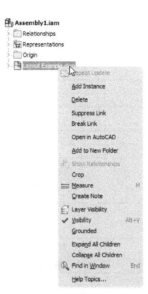

Figure 5–5

**Hint: Associative DWG Underlays in Drawings**

To include a DWG underlay in a drawing view, right-click on the Associative DWG file associated with the view and select **Include**, as shown in Figure 5–6. Once included, you can add text, dimensions, manage layers, or edit line types to appropriately annotate the underlay geometry.

Figure 5–6

**Hint: AutoCAD Mechanical files as DWG Underlays**

AutoCAD Mechanical files can be imported as DWG files. If imported into an assembly file, constraints can be used to constrain the drawing. Note that cropped AutoCAD Mechanical geometry cannot be selected. Do not crop the DWG file.

## Practice 5a

# Import Associative DWG Data into a Part File

### Practice Objective

- Open an AutoCAD DWG file directly into an Autodesk Inventor part file and work with the data.

In this practice, you will import an AutoCAD DWG file into an Autodesk Inventor file as an underlay. You will control the layer visibility and its location in the file so that the underlay can be used to project geometry onto sketches. The sketch geometry will then be used to create a 3D model. The geometry that will be created is shown in Figure 5–7.

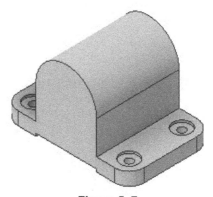

**Figure 5–7**

### Task 1 - Create a new Autodesk Inventor model and import AutoCAD data.

1. Start a new part file using the **Standard (in).ipt** template.

2. Save the file as **AssociativeDWG.ipt**. A DWG file cannot be imported into a new, unsaved file.

3. In the *3D Model* tab>Create panel, click ⊞ (Import).

4. In the Import dialog box, expand the Files of type drop-down list and select **AutoCAD DWG Files (*.dwg)**.

5. Select **YA-Base.dwg** from the practice files folder and click **Open**.

6. Select the XY Origin plane as the plane to import the DWG file to.

7. Select the projected Origin Center Point as the centerpoint for the import.

8. Click **OK** when prompted that inserting an AutoCAD DWG produces an associative underlay.

9. Review the three 2D views. Note that the side view is a section view.

## Task 2 - Set the Layer Visibility on the AutoCAD DWG file.

1. Right-click on **YA-Base.dwg** in the Model browser and select **Layer Visibility**. The Layer Visibility dialog box opens.

2. In the filter settings at the top of the dialog box, click

   (Clear All) to clear all the layers from being displayed.

3. Select **YA-Base|Hidden Edges**, **YA-Base|Tangent Edges**, and **YA-Base|Visible Edges**.

4. Click **OK** to close the Layer Visibility dialog box. The visibility of any of the layers can be controlled at any time using this dialog box.

## Task 3 - Crop the AutoCAD DWG file.

1. Right-click on **YA-Base.dwg** in the Model browser and select **Crop**.

2. Drag a bounding box around the two views shown in Figure 5–8. The box defines which entities in the underlay file will remain in the file.

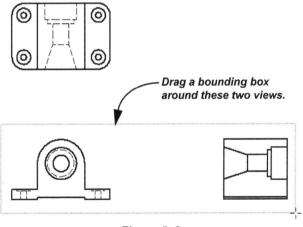

*Drag a bounding box around these two views.*

**Figure 5–8**

3. Right-click and select **OK (Enter)** to remove the entities outside the bounding box from view.

---

**Task 4 - Translate the AutoCAD DWG file relative to the model's origin.**

---

1. Expand the **Origin** node in the Model browser and toggle on the visibility of the Center Point.

2. Using the Navigation Bar, select **Zoom All** to refit the model so that both the Origin Center Point and the drawing are displayed on the screen. If you are using a white background you may have difficulty seeing the yellow origin center point. Hover the cursor over the origin planes in the Model Browser to display them in the model to understand where the origin point is located.

3. Right-click on **YA-Base.dwg** in the Model browser and select **Translate**.

4. A triad displays on the Origin Center Point. Click **Locate** in the mini-toolbar. Select the center point of the internal hole, as shown in Figure 5–9.

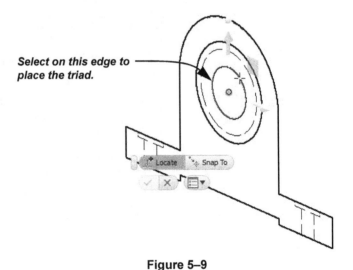

Select on this edge to place the triad.

Figure 5–9

5. Click ✓ to close the mini-toolbar and complete the translation.

6. Return the model to its Home View using the ViewCube.

---

## Task 5 - Create associative geometry from the DWG file.

1. Create a new 2D sketch on the XY plane.

2. In the *Sketch* tab>Create panel, expand the Project Geometry options and select ![icon] (Project DWG Geometry).

3. In the mini-toolbar, select ![icon] (Project Connected Geometry) and select on an outside edge in the Front view, as shown on the left in Figure 5–10. All connected edges are projected. Project the outside loop of single edges on the section view, as shown on the right of Figure 5–10.

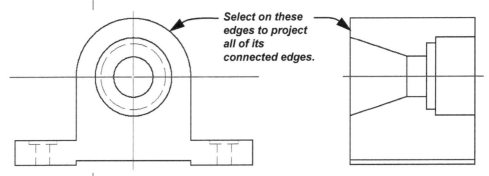

*Select on these edges to project all of its connected edges.*

**Figure 5–10**

4. Click ![X icon] to close the mini-toolbar and cancel the Project DWG Geometry command.

5. Create a dimension in the side section view to define the depth of the model. Once placed, you will be prompted that the dimension will over-constrain the sketch. Click **Accept** to place the dimension as a Driven Dimension, as shown in Figure 5–11.

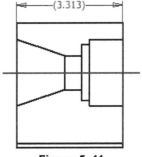

**Figure 5–11**

6. Finish the sketch.

7. Right-click in the graphics window and click **Dimension Display>Name** to display the name of the dimension value.

8. Create an Extrude and select the section shown in Figure 5–12. Enter **d0** (or name of your Driven Dimension) as the value for the extruded depth.

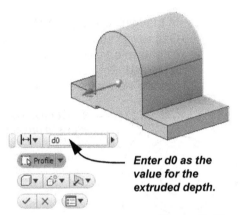

*Enter d0 as the value for the extruded depth.*

**Figure 5–12**

9. Complete the feature.

---

### Task 6 - Insert the DWG on another plane and create additional geometry.

---

1. In the *3D Model* tab>Create panel, click 🔁 (Import).

2. In the Import dialog box, select **YA-Base.dwg** from the practice files folder and click **Open**.

3. Select the plane and origin point shown in Figure 5–13 as the references to import the DWG file.

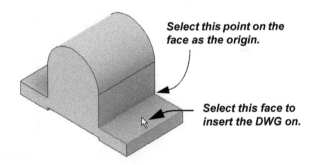

*Select this point on the face as the origin.*

*Select this face to insert the DWG on.*

**Figure 5–13**

---

4. When prompted that inserting an AutoCAD DWG produces an associative underlay, click **OK**.

5. Right-click on the newly imported **YA-Base.dwg** in the Model browser and select **Layer Visibility**. The Layer Visibility dialog box opens. Note that the same visibility settings are set. Click **OK** to close the Layer Visibility dialog box.

6. In the Navigation Bar, select **Zoom All** to refit the model to see the solid geometry and the new underlay.

7. Right-click on newly imported **YA-Base.dwg** in the Model browser and select **Translate**.

8. A triad appears, by default, on the point that was selected on the placement face. Click **Locate** in the mini-toolbar. Select the point shown in Figure 5–14 on the newly imported underlay.

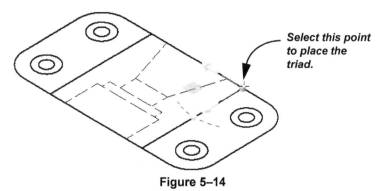

**Figure 5–14**

9. Click ✔ to close the mini-toolbar and complete the translation.

10. Both underlays are on different planes and are visible. Right-click on the first **YA-Base.dwg** and clear the **Visibility** option. You can toggle the display of underlays on and off as required.

11. Create a new sketch on the same face that was used to place the latest DWG underlay file.

12. In the Create panel, click (Project DWG Geometry).

13. In the mini-toolbar, ensure that (Project Single Geometry) is selected and select the four arcs on the outside corners of the view shown in Figure 5–15 to project them.

14. Project one large and one small circle, as shown in Figure 5–15. Close the mini-toolbar or cancel the command.

15. Create the three Driven Dimensions shown in Figure 5–15.

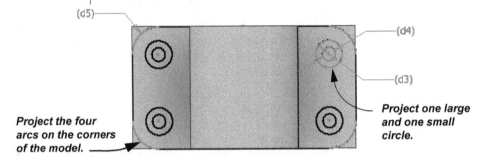

**Figure 5–15**

16. While in the same sketch, project the required edges and create the reference dimension shown in Figure 5–16.

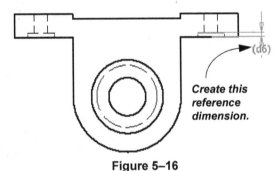

**Figure 5–16**

17. Finish the sketch.

18. Create a Fillet.

*The dimension name may vary depending on the order that you created the Driven Dimensions in the sketch.*

19. Select the four vertical edges on the outside of the model. Enter **d5** (or name of your Driven Dimension) as the value of the fillet, as shown in Figure 5–17. This ensures the size of the fillet is driven by the projected geometry.

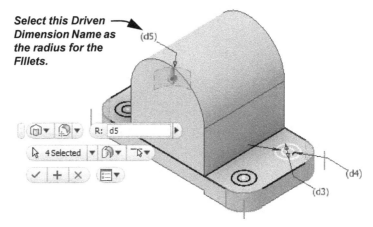

Figure 5–17

20. Complete the feature.

21. Create a Hole. Select **Concentric** as the placement type.

22. Change the hole type to **Counterbore** and select the placement plane and concentric references shown in Figure 5–18.

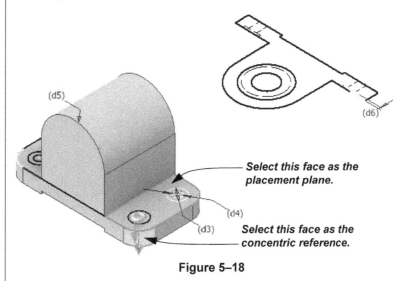

Figure 5–18

23. Enter the dimension values for the hole using the Driven Dimensions that were created in the sketch, as shown in Figure 5–19. Ensure that you enter the correct dimension name to match the counterbore dimensions. Create the hole as **Through All**.

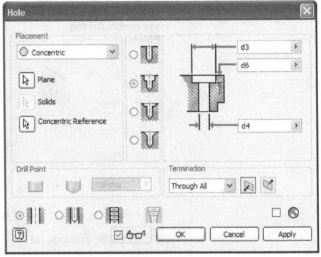

Figure 5–19

24. Complete the feature.

25. Create the additional three counterbore holes using the Concentric option and the same Driven Dimensions.

26. Toggle off the visibility of the second imported DWG underlay and the sketch. The model displays as shown in Figure 5–20.

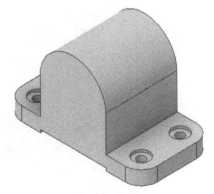

Figure 5–20

27. Save the file.

## Task 7 - Replace the YA-Base.dwg with a modified version.

1. Open Windows Explorer and navigate to the practice files folder.

2. Rename **YA-Base.dwg** to **YA-Base_Original.dwg**.

3. Rename **YA-Base_Updated.dwg** to **YA-Base.dwg**. This new file has had changes made to the file to increase the size of the holes and the depth of the model.

4. Return to Autodesk Inventor and review the **AssociativeDWG.ipt**. The Model browser indicates that **YA-Base.dwg** has been updated, as shown by the lightening bolt icons in Figure 5–21.

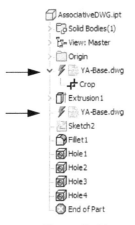

**Figure 5–21**

5. In the Quick Access toolbar, select 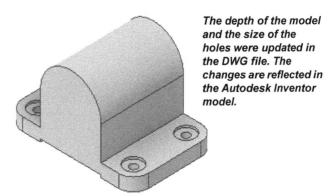 (Local Update). Note that the model updates as shown in Figure 5–22.

*The depth of the model and the size of the holes were updated in the DWG file. The changes are reflected in the Autodesk Inventor model.*

**Figure 5–22**

6. In the Model Browser, right-click on either of the **YA-Base.dwg** files and note the **Suppress Link** and **Break Link** options. These options can be used to either temporarily break the link with the source DWG file (**Suppress Link**) or permanently break the link (**Break Link**).

7. Save the model and close the window.

### Optional Task - Continue modeling the solid geometry.

After you have finished creating all of the practices in this chapter, continue to add the geometry from the DWG file into the Autodesk Inventor model. The only remaining feature is a revolved cut. To create this, consider creating a workplane and project the section that is to be revolved. Alternatively, edit one of the sketches and add more Driven Dimensions that can be used to drive additional hole features.

# Practice 5b | Associative DWG Layout

### Practice Objectives

- Import an AutoCAD .DWG file as an underlay in an Autodesk Inventor part file.
- Assemble the underlay part file as the base grounded component and reference it to place and create components.

In this practice, you will begin by creating a new part file that imports an AutoCAD DWG file for use as an underlay. The underlay is imported so that associativity is maintained between the files. The part file is then used in an assembly to constrain and create new components in the assembly. To complete the practice, a change is made in the original DWG file and the updates are shown to reflect in the assembly file. The geometry that will be created is shown in Figure 5–23.

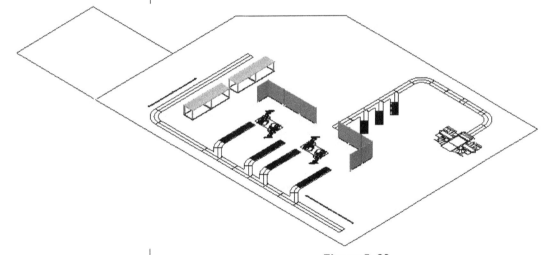

**Figure 5–23**

**Note:** With the release of the Autodesk Inventor 2018 software (March 2017) you are now able to place a DWG underlay directly into an assembly. This release does not provide an option to Translate the underlay, as is available in the Part environment. To rotate on the placement plane, you can edit the **Angle 2** constraint in the **Relationships** folder. This exercise requires you to translate the placement point so that the underlay will be referenced through a part file (as was the process in the 2017 software release).

## Task 1 - Create a new Autodesk Inventor model and import AutoCAD data.

1. Start a new part file using the **Standard (in).ipt** template.

2. A DWG file cannot be imported into a new, unsaved file. Save the new file as **FactoryLayout.ipt**.

3. In the *3D Model* tab>Create panel, click ⬁ (Import).

4. In the Import dialog box, expand the Files of type drop-down list and select **AutoCAD DWG Files (*.dwg)**.

5. Select **Layout Example.dwg** from the practice files folder and click **Open**.

6. Select the XZ Origin plane as the plane to import the DWG file.

7. Select the projected Origin Center Point as the centerpoint for the import.

8. Click **OK** when prompted that inserting an AutoCAD DWG produces an associative underlay.

9. Review the factory layout. The orientation of the drawing should be rotated 180 degrees and the origin point needs to be repositioned. In the next task you will reorient the imported DWG file.

## Task 2 - Translate the AutoCAD DWG file relative to the model's origin.

1. Expand the **Origin** node in the Model browser. Toggle on the visibility of the Center Point and note where it is located.

2. Right-click on **Layout Example.dwg** in the Model browser and select **Translate**.

3. A triad displays on the Origin Center Point. Select the rotation handle shown in Figure 5–24 to enable the rotation of the imported DWG file.

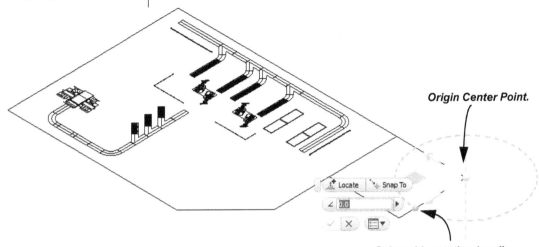

*Origin Center Point.*

*Select this rotation handle
(gray dot) to enable rotation.*

**Figure 5–24**

4.  Enter **180** to rotate the DWG file.

5.  Click **Locate** in the mini-toolbar and select the point where
    the two rooms join, as shown in Figure 5–25.

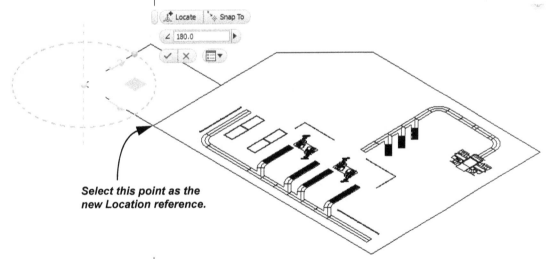

*Select this point as the
new Location reference.*

**Figure 5–25**

6.  Click **Snap To** in the mini-toolbar and select the Origin Center
    Point in the Model browser to align the DWG underlay and
    the reference point on the drawing.

7. Click 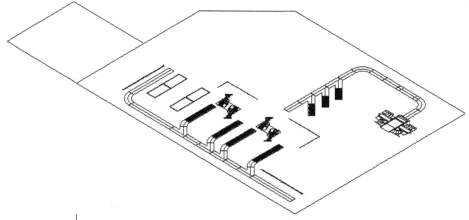 to close the mini-toolbar and complete the translation. The model should display as shown in Figure 5–26.

**Figure 5–26**

## Task 3 - Set the Layer Visibility for the AutoCAD DWG file.

1. Right-click on **Layout Example.dwg** in the Model browser and select **Layer Visibility**. The Layer Visibility dialog box opens. This dialog box enables you to control the DWG layers that are displayed in the Autodesk Inventor model.

2. Select **Layout Example|Slab** in the list and note how additional entities are added to the view. As these are not required, you can leave this option cleared.

3. Select **Layout Example|Walls-Interior** to clear the option. Note how all of the entities are cleared. In this drawing all of the entities have been added to this layer. Select **Layout Example|Walls-Interior** again to enable the option.

4. Click **OK** to close the Layer Visibility dialog box. The visibility of layers can be controlled at any time using this dialog box.

5. Save the model.

## Task 4 - Use the associative DWG file as a reference for assembling and creating components in an assembly.

1. Start a new assembly file using the **Standard (in).iam** template.

2. Place one instance of **FactoryLayout.ipt** into the assembly file. Right-click and select **Place Grounded at Origin** to assemble the part as the base model and ground it.

3. Press <Esc> to cancel the assembly of additional instances of the **FactoryLayout.ipt** file.

4. Place a single instance of **Table.iam** into the assembly file, as shown in Figure 5–27.

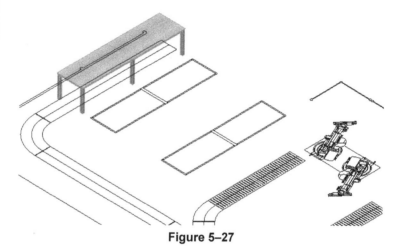

**Figure 5–27**

5. In the *Assembly* tab>Relationships panel, click

    (Constrain).

6. Using the Place Constraint dialog box, assign the following constraints to fully locate the table relative to the **FactoryLayout.ipt** file:

- Mate the XZ plane of the table component to the XZ plane of the assembly. Use the **Flush** orientation.
- Add two Mate constraints that align the edges of the table legs and the border of the table's layout in the X and Z directions, as shown in Figure 5–28.

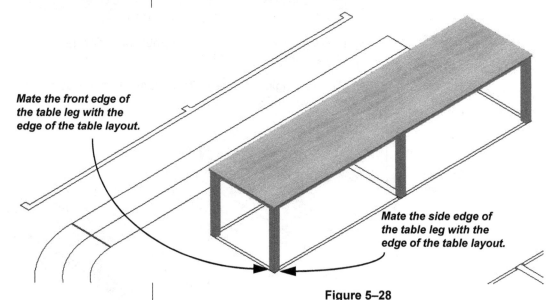

*Mate the front edge of the table leg with the edge of the table layout.*

*Mate the side edge of the table leg with the edge of the table layout.*

**Figure 5–28**

7. Close the Place Constraints dialog box.

8. Place a second instance of **Table.iam** and constrain it to the other table layout. The final assembly should display as shown in Figure 5–29.

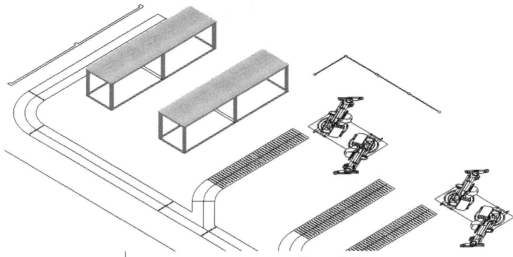

**Figure 5–29**

9. Save the file as **Factory.iam**.

---

**Task 5 - Create part geometry using the AutoCAD DWG underlay as a reference.**

---

1. In the *Assembly* tab>Component panel, click ⬜ (Create) to start a new part file in the context of the assembly.

2. In the Create In-Place Component dialog box, enter **Screen.ipt** as the name of the new file and assign **Standard(in).ipt** as the part template to be used. Click **OK**.

3. Select the XZ plane of the assembly as the sketch plane reference for the new part. **Screen.ipt** becomes the active component in the assembly (if not, activate it).

4. In the *3D Model* tab>Sketch panel, click ▱ (Start 2D Sketch).

5. Select the XY plane in the Screen model as the sketching plane for the sketch.

6. In the *Sketch* tab>Create panel, expand the **Project Geometry** option, and select ⬚ (Project DWG Geometry).

7. In the mini-toolbar, ensure that 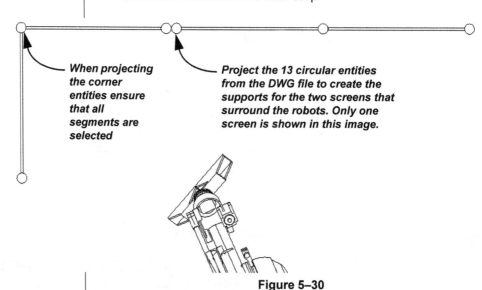 (Project Single Geometry) is selected. Select the 13 circular entities described in Figure 5–30. If the entire entity is not selected, it cannot be extruded in a later step.

*When projecting the corner entities ensure that all segments are selected*

*Project the 13 circular entities from the DWG file to create the supports for the two screens that surround the robots. Only one screen is shown in this image.*

**Figure 5–30**

8. Finish the sketch and rename the sketch as **Supports**.

9. Create a second sketch on the XY plane and start the (Project DWG Geometry) option.

10. In the mini-toolbar, select ⬜ (Project Connected Geometry) and project the 9 rectangles that are used to define the screen geometry between the supports, as shown in Figure 5–31.

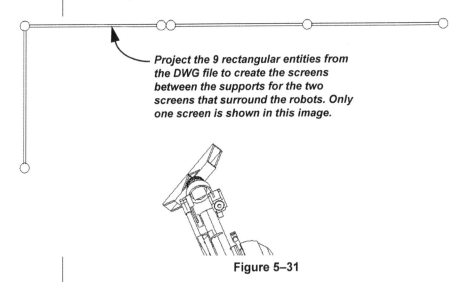

*Project the 9 rectangular entities from the DWG file to create the screens between the supports for the two screens that surround the robots. Only one screen is shown in this image.*

Figure 5–31

11. Finish the sketch and rename the sketch as **Screens**.

12. Use the **Extrude** command to create the screen geometry shown in Figure 5–32.

- Extrude the 13 circular entities in the Supports sketch to a height of **72 in**.
- Extrude the 9 rectangular entities in the Screens sketch to a height of **70 in**.

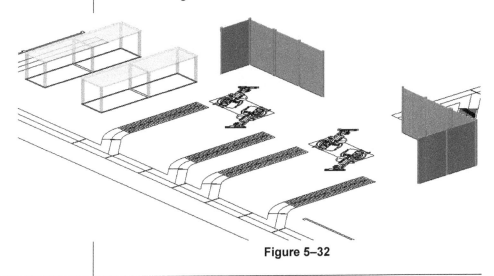

Figure 5–32

13. Reactivate the top-level assembly.

14. Save the assembly and the newly created part file.

## Task 6 - Update the DWG underlay and the associated geometry.

1. Open Windows Explorer and navigate to the practice files folder.

2. Rename **Layout Example.dwg** to **Layout Example_OLD.dwg**.

3. Rename **Layout Example_Updated.dwg** to **Layout Example.dwg**. This new file has had changes made to the file to relocate the tables and change the size of one of the screens.

4. Return to Autodesk Inventor and note that the 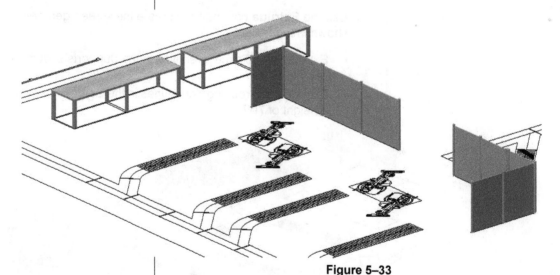 (Local Update) option is available in the Quick Access toolbar and that the **FactoryLayout** underlay is showing as out-of-date in the Model Browser. Click (Local Update) to update the assembly, as shown in Figure 5–33.

**Figure 5–33**

5. Save the assembly and close the files.

# Chapter Review Questions

6. Which of the following are true statements regarding importing AutoCAD DWG data as an underlay into an Autodesk Inventor model? (Select all that apply.)

   a. The DWG data can only be imported onto a single plane in the model.

   b. The layers in the DWG underlay can be set to display only specific layers.

   c. Use the **Project Geometry** command to project and use DWG data in a sketch.

   d. The DWG data that is imported remains unassociated with the source data.

   e. The visibility of the DWG underlays can be controlled using the **Visibility** option.

7. Which of the following best describes how the **Translate** command can be used? (Select all that apply.)

   a. The **Translate** command enables you to relocate the DWG underlay on the same plane.

   b. The **Translate** command enables you to relocate the DWG underlay onto another plane.

   c. The **Translate** command enables you to snap the DWG underlay to the origin center point on the same plane.

8. You can crop an imported DWG underlay in multiple locations to simplify the data that displays.

   a. True

   b. False

9. When using a DWG underlay in an Autodesk Inventor file, which of the following statements are true? (Select all that apply.)

   a. Use the **Project Geometry** option to project the DWG entities into a sketch.

   b. Once imported, the link between the DWG entities and created geometry can be temporarily suppressed using the **Break Link** option.

   c. An imported AutoCAD DWG file can also be used as a layout reference to assemble components.

   d. An imported AutoCAD DWG file can be displayed in a drawing view of the Inventor file.

**Answers:** 1.(b,e), 2.(a,c), 3.b, 4.(c,d)

# Command Summary

| Button | Command | Location |
|--------|---------|----------|
| | **Import** | • **Ribbon:** *3D Model* tab>Create panel |
| | **Project DWG Geometry** | • **Ribbon:** *Sketch* tab>Create panel |

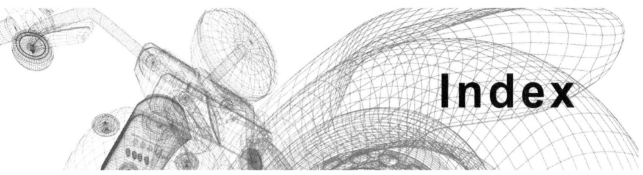

# Index

www.ingramcontent.com/pod-product-compliance
Lightning Source LLC
Chambersburg PA
CBHW080419060326
40689CB00019B/4305